The Challenges for New Principals in the Twenty-First Century

Developing Leadership Capabilities Through Professional Support

A volume in
International Research on School Leadership

Series Editors:
Alan R. Shoho, Bruce G. Barnett,
University of Texas at San Antonio
Autumn K. Tooms,
University of Tennessee

International Research on School Leadership

Alan R. Shoho, Bruce G. Barnett, and Autumn K. Tooms, Series Editors

The Challenges for New Principals in the Twenty-First Century

Developing Leadership Capabilities Through Professional Support

edited by

Alan R. Shoho
University of Texas at San Antonio

Bruce G.Barnett
University of Texas at San Antonio

and

Autumn K. Tooms
Kent State University

Information Age Publishing, Inc.
Charlotte, North Carolina • www.infoagepub.com

Library of Congress Cataloging-in-Publication Data

The challenges for new principals in the twenty-first century : developing
leadership capabilities through professional support / edited by Alan R.
Shoho, Bruce Barnett, Autumn Tooms.
    p. cm. -- (International research on school leadership)
  Includes bibliographical references and index.
  ISBN 978-1-61735-092-4 (pbk.) -- ISBN 978-1-61735-093-1 (hardcover) --
ISBN 978-1-61735-094-8 (e-book)
  1. Educational leadership--United States. 2. School principals--United
States. 3. School improvement programs--United States. I. Shoho, Alan R.
II. Barnett, Bruce. III. Tooms, Autumn, 1965-

  LB2805.C424 2010
  371.2'.012--dc22

2010021952

Printed in the United States of America

CONTENTS

ACKNOWLEDGMENTS

Like any peer-reviewed publication, the contributions of many people beyond the authors and coeditors are critical to the development of an edited book. As coeditors, we want to recognize the invaluable contributions our peer reviewers made for reviewing manuscripts and providing substantive feedback. Their feedback allowed the authors to refine their manuscripts and make meaningful contributions to the work of new principals or headteachers in schools.

Tom Alsbury, North Carolina State University
Peggy Basom, San Diego State University
Paul Begley, Nipissing University
Alex Bowers, University of Texas at San Antonio
Gary Crow, Indiana University
Dan Duke, University of Virginia
Fenwick English, University of North Carolina at Chapel Hill
Tricia Ferrigno-Brown, University of Kentucky
Bonnie Fusarelli, North Carolina State University
Jeff Goldhorn, Education Region Service Center 20, San Antonio, TX
Don Hackmann, University of Illinois at Urbana–Champaign
Gene Hall, University of Nevada, Las Vegas
Joann Klinker, Texas Tech University
Betty Murakami-Ramalho, University of Texas at San Antonio
Karen Osterman, Hofstra University
Tom Parks, University of Texas at Permian Basin
George Petersen, California Polytechnic University, San Luis Obispo
Cindy Reed, Auburn University

Rick Reitzug, University of North Carolina at Greensboro
Mariela Rodriguez, University of Texas at San Antonio
Bill Ruff, University of Montana
Charlie Slater, California State University at Long Beach
Howard Stevenson, University of Lincoln
Cynthia Stone, South San Antonio Independent School District
Ross Thomas, University of Wollongong
David Thompson, University of Texas at San Antonio
Elaine Wilmore, University of Texas at Permian Basin

Our thanks to photographer Mark McClendon, University of Texas at San Antonio for contributing the book cover photo. We would also like to acknowledge the principals depicted in the book cover photo: Tallest man is Mr. Stanley Laing, Principal of Tom Clark High School in San Antonio, Texas; African American man is Mr. Anthony Jarrett, Principal of John Marshall High School in San Antonio, Texas; blond lady is Dr. Geri Berger, Principal of Louis Brandeis High School in San Antonio, Texas; and darker haired lady is Mrs. Jacqueline Horras, Principal of Sandra Day O'Connor High School in San Antonio, Texas.

INTRODUCTION

Alan R. Shoho, Bruce G. Barnett, and Autumn K. Tooms

This book series, *International Research on School Leadership,* focuses on how present-day issues affect the theory and practice of school leadership. For this inaugural book, we focused on the challenges facing new principals and headteachers. Because the professional lives of school leaders have increasingly impinged on their personal well-being and resources have continued to shrink, it is important to understand how new principals or headteachers share and divide their energy, ideas, and time within the school day. It is also important to discover ways to provide professional development and support for new principals and headteachers as they strive to lead their schools in the twenty-first century. For these reasons, this book is dedicated to exploring the rarely examined experiences of those who enter the role as new principals or headteachers. By giving voice to new principals and headteachers, we are able to determine what aspects of leadership preparation ring true and what aspects prove to be of little or no utility. Unlike leadership texts that have focused on conceptual considerations and personal narratives from the field, this book focuses on a collection of empirical efforts centered on the challenges and issues that new principals and headteachers experience during their initial and crucial years of induction. We solicited and accepted manuscripts that explore the multifaceted dimensions of being a new principal or headteacher in the twenty-first century. Our goal was to create an edited book that examines the commonalities and differences that new principals and headteachers experience from an international perspective. This edited book is comprised of six chapters, each of which contributes a unique perspective on the responsibilities that new principals and head-teachers are experiencing at the dawn of the twenty-first century.

In Chapter 1 "Translational Leadership: New Principals and the Theory and Practice of School Leadership in the Twenty-First Century," Fusarelli, Militello, Alsbury, Price, and Warren explore the evolution of theory and practice of school leadership and how this shift affects new principals. Drawing from data collected from a Q-sort research study and from a qualitative case study of one first-year principal, the authors illustrate how new school leaders are expected to be *translational leaders*.

Alsbury (2009) elaborated, "translational leadership" is a term adopted from the medical field to illustrate an approach to translate medical research and theory to patient care and application (i.e., tying theory to practice). Translational leaders do not rely solely on a one-size-fits-all set of educational leadership practices but must apply relevant contextual diversity in their individual school community to generic standards-based practice. As a result, principals translate the standards as they decide how to prioritize their time and divide their energy within the school day. As the authors illustrate, these decisions are often difficult because of conflicting demands on their time. This is particularly true for new principals who are expected to be experts from day one, despite the fact that they have a steep learning curve and are being pushed and pulled from a variety of sources.

Using translational leadership as their conceptual lenses, Fusarelli and colleagues found that new principals tend to prioritize and operationalize some, but not all leadership standards. One of the conclusions drawn from this study is that despite the field's efforts to standardize leadership practices (i.e., through ISLLC and ELCC standards), new principals tend to customize a mixture of leadership practices based on contextual and personal factors. This finding supports the notion that twenty-first century leadership requires principals to translate espoused theories and adopted standards to relevant practices in their given environment. Translational leadership also provides insight into reframing leadership preparation programs to emphasize "right-brain" and emotional intelligence skills to enable new principals to formulate responsive actions to nonstandardized situations. This is an appropriate segue to the next two chapters that focus on new headteachers in England and Uganda and the cultural contexts associated with leadership practices.

In their chapter, "New Headteachers in Schools in England and Their Approaches to Leadership," Forrester and Gunter describe the changing realities confronting new headteachers as government policies demand schools be more accountable for student performance. The current political context in England requires headteachers and their schools to emphasize basic subjects and meet performance targets, while being subjected to constant monitoring and inspection. This study is part of a larger investigation of headteachers involved in the nationally funded Knowledge Production in Educational Leadership Project. The chapter focuses on how novice headteachers learn and adapt their leadership approaches. The sample consists of nine primary and secondary headteachers who recently completed the government-sponsored National Professional Qualification for Headteachers (NPQH), are in their first 5 years of headship, and are located in various geographical regions and socioeconomic areas across England.

Forrester and Gunter's research contributes to our understanding of the significant professional and organizational socialization processes novices experience prior to and during their initial experiences as headteachers. In addition, important findings and implications for leadership preparation and development for new headteachers are reported. The analysis reveals novices use several leadership approaches, including directive (i.e., leading based on their headteacher position), distributed (i.e., delegating responsibility for tasks and accountability), and inclusive (i.e., building community through personal relationships). Demonstrating the evolving and contextual nature of leadership, the authors provide examples of how these new headteachers initially rely on the directive approach before adopting an inclusive style. The study also reveals important learning experiences shaping novices' views and actions as leaders. Similar to other studies, these beginning headteachers were strongly influenced by significant role models (teachers, deputies, and headteachers); however, they also reported important contributions of their formal NPQH training, acknowledging the hands-on experiences that helped build their self-confidence and clarify their leadership philosophies.

One of the unique aspects of the study is how novices contend with the legacies of their predecessors. In some cases, novices replaced headteachers who had been at the school for over 20 years. Replacing these school leaders pose significant challenges because teachers, staff, and community members are familiar and comfortable with how the school is run, expectations about their role in decision making, and the direction of the school. Illustrations are provided of the challenges these new heads face when dealing with dominating parents, confronting incompetent teachers, and working with deputy headteachers who were unsuccessful in obtaining the job.

The notion that professional vulnerability increases exponentially with one's ascension in an organization is not new; however, Chapter 3, written by Hallam, Hite, Hite, and Mugimu," "So You Want to be a Headteacher?: 'Liabilities of Newness,' Challenges, and Strategies of New Headteachers in Uganda," reminds us that this paradox rampantly runs within the discourses of school leadership in the nation of Uganda. Like many education systems in both developed and developing countries, the discussions of rigor slam directly into the pressures of economy. This plays out in everyday ways unique to Uganda's postcolonial society. Mazrui and Klaben (1986) noted that the macro- and socioeconomic politics of Uganda exemplify a solid critique of Marxist intentions inherently fostered in the postcolonial era. As Marx put it, "And so the ultimate power resides not in those who control the means of production, as Marxists would argue, but rather in the hands of those who control the means of destruction" (as cited in Mazrui & Klaben, 1986, p. 166). Thus, what is most common in modern Ugandan society is an inextricable link between European policies and practices (that have more cultural capital) from more realistic and indigenous needs and discourses (Mazrui & Klaben, 1986). Such is the case with how schools are funded, supported, and led throughout Uganda.

Hallam and colleagues open their discussion of the above tensions with a brief explanation of how the Ugandan system is structured. We learn that the hallmarks of the Ugandan education system include a relatively loose infrastructure in which the majority of schools are not funded by the government. Funding is not related to a school's status as public or private, religious or secular. Thus, the need for tuition funds drives a market economy in school systems that seeps into the day-to-day leadership decisions of those who manage schools. In particular, this forms a tension between the headteacher who is charged with the direct and day-to-day leadership of a school, and his or her immediate supervisor, the director. Juxtaposed against this tension are the wants and tuition funds of parents whose children attend (and can leave) the school. The resulting dynamic is a dysfunctional system in which the headteacher can find his or her leadership decisions trumped by the director's desire to acquiesce to parents in order to ensure a stable flow of tuition dollars. Compounding this issue are the micropolitical nuances of the socialization process for new headteachers. This study revealed that the liabilities for those who are new to the position of headteacher could be described in five ways: (1) the politics of succession process, (2) role ambiguity, (3) limited resources, (4) balancing diverse stakeholders needs, and (5) ensuring high student performance. To address these challenges, headteachers employed several strategies, including the active pursuit of advice from a variety of mentors and colleagues, diligently communicating with school stakeholders, and consistently looking to build bridges that would enhance the school image. The implications of this study aim directly at the Ugandan Ministry of Education, who is called upon to better support those new to the role of headteacher. Training should address specific educational context, the educational system as a whole, the influences of community and economy, and most importantly the importance for establishing clear roles and responsibilities.

What remains to be seen is the ability of the Ministry of Education to implement more threads of infrastructure throughout the Ugandan education system. While this chapter certainly focuses on one study that centered on one district, some lessons for the Ugandan Education system are revealed. Like most challenges in education systems, they are messy, not always obvious, woven within politics and economy, and will take a long time to solve.

In contrast to developing an educational system with the appropriate infrastructure that Uganda is experiencing, the next chapter, by Woodruff and Kowalski, "Problems Reported by Novice High School Principals," focuses on the challenges encountered by novice high school principals in the United States where issues of infrastructure and system are well-established. Despite the advancement of the American educational system, there are still numerous challenges facing novice principals.

While there is a healthy amount of research dedicated to the processes and structures embedded in principal induction, very little attention is devoted to the perspectives of novice principals. Woodruff and Kowalski address this gap in the literature in two interesting ways. First, they utilize the research that is the heart of their chapter as a way to focus tightly on the viewpoint of novice high school principals. They define novices as those who have just completed their first year in the role. Second, the authors employ a quantitative methodology in their effort, something not prevalent within inquiries dedicated to discussions of induction, socialization, politics, and novice school administrators. The sample used for this effort was located in Ohio, a state planted firmly in the midwestern United States known for its yeasty politics and neoconservative approach to education, despite the many pockets of liberals (and thus liberal school systems) inherent in its geography.

Woodruff and Kowalski capture the views of novices as a mechanism to articulate the nature and frequency of problems found in daily practices as related to the demographic variables of school. The justification for this lens is centered on a recognition of policymakers' belief that most school administrators have failed to apply empirical evidence to their practice (Kowalski, 2009). While research has demonstrated that principals experience anxiety, frustration, alienation, and self-doubt, scant efforts explore how these vexing emotions are related to specific challenges of practice and school demographics.

It has been argued that the gathering of stories and insights (i.e., a qualitative epistemology) produces thick descriptions of reality, something typically desired in the study of what it is like to be in the role of principal, novice or otherwise. However, quantitative measures such as survey instruments have their value and place within this line of inquiry. And these authors make a nimble case for such considerations. The survey instrument was created specifically for this study and was circulated to 25 novice principals in the state of Ohio. Obtaining an impressive response rate (84%), the instrument's internal consistency also was high (.95). Descriptive analysis revealed similarities with existing literature. For example, novice high school principals in the sample were typical and congruent with national trends in the United States in terms of what a novice high school principal looks like (Alvy & Coladarci, 1985; National Association of Secondary School Principals, 2001): They are usually male, Anglo, in their mid-40s, with slightly more than a decade of teaching experience. In addition, novice principals tended to struggle with instructional supervision as well as other managerial responsibilities.

What is interesting is that the novice principals in this study confirmed the multiplicity of personal challenges/problems previously noted in the literature. Examples of these include the job's stress on the family and inadequate compensation, time, and workload. This speaks volumes as to the importance of supporting and mentoring novices in ways that are deeper than tertiary workshops on time management and student discipline. The chapter begs for recognition of the damning nature of the role of new leader, especially within the context of high-problem schools and instructional leadership. And because this study demonstrated that novices who had experience in schools were more conscious of challenges to school improvement, there are undeniable implications related to alternative certification for school leaders. In other words, Woodruff and Kowalski have deftly shown us that it is completely illogical to allow for policies and practices (such as alternative certifications and online programs) that endorse the placement of novice principals in schools that have little or no experience outside of the classroom.

Given the challenges facing new principals and headteachers highlighted by Forrester and Gunter, Hallam and colleagues, and Woodruff and Kowalski, it is impertinent for school districts and universities to develop new ways to provide meaningful support. In Chapter 5, "Accelerating New Principal Development Through Leadership Coaching," Lochmiller and Silver advance the purposeful coaching model as a tactic to help new principals develop the knowledge and skills needed to facilitate successful instructional practices in classrooms.

In their study, Lochmiller and Silver found that the top three challenges facing new principals according to their coaches were observing classroom instruction, conducting learning walks, and writing effective teacher evaluations. The key issue was that new principals needed a firm foundation of what effective instruction looked like as well as the capacity to provide timely and meaningful feedback to teachers about their instructional practices. One of the key questions that all principals (new or experienced) must address is: To what degree are teachers taking personal responsibility for their students' learning?

The purposeful coaching model is one way to answer this question by providing trained coaches to support new principals by gathering evidence, asking questions, managing reflection, and monitoring action. As Lochmiller and Silver noted,

> leadership coaches provided substantial support for the new principals by gathering evidence about the new principals' practice or the schools' needs, asking them questions about their leadership action or the conditions they identified, and helping the new principals reflect on their leadership practice. Each of these activities aided new principals to focus their leadership with laser-like precision on instructional practices and ways to improve student learning in their schools.

Two methods employed by coaches to assist new principals was the use of videotaping of staff meetings and teacher focus groups whereby the coach conducted a modified version of a 360-degree assessment of the principal's leadership. The videotape illustrated to new principals the reality that they were not addressing instruction as much as they thought they were. And the modified 360-degree assessment helped new principals to "calibrate" and check how their actions were being interpreted by their teachers. Through activities such as videotaping and teacher focus groups, leadership coaches were able to assist new principals in developing an "instructional routine." The authors describe an instructional routine as the work of instructional leadership within a framework for new principals to gather their "sea" legs as they navigate through the throes of learning the principalship during the first year. As part of the instructional routine, the coaches identified the development of effective teacher evaluations and constructive feedback as one of the most important aspects of the process.

Given the value reported by new principals for leadership coaches, Lochmiller and Silver conclude by noting "leadership coaching may accelerate principal development as instructional leaders" There seems to be little doubt that having a supportive coach to bounce ideas and reflect on decisions and instructional practices was found to be of paramount value to new principals in their study. The question remains, however, are school districts and universities willing to explore ways to support new principals or will they continue to have the attitude, "let them figure it out themselves?"

The final chapter of this book on new principals and headteachers complements the work of Lochmiller and Silver's chapter, focusing on a large school district's efforts to provide mentoring and coaching to all new principals. The evolution of a district-initiated mentoring and coaching program for first-time principals in the Chicago Public Schools (CPS) is highlighted in John Daresh's chapter, "From Mentoring to Coaching: Finding the Path to Support for Beginning Principals." This support program for beginning principals was part of the Effective Leaders Improve Schools (ELIS) Project, funded by the U.S. Department of Education, the City of Chicago, and the Wallace Foundation. The chapter chronicles the ELIS Project's first 3 years and highlights the contributions of the Office of Principal Preparation and Development (OPPD), a professional development unit dedicated to improving the quality of principal candidates, selecting outstanding principals, and supporting beginning and experienced principals' success. ELIS not only is intended to prepare and assist novice school administrators, but also to shift the image of CPS principals from building managers to instructional leaders. The importance of ELIS is critical because the CPS system was hiring over 100 new principals each year of the project.

Although most descriptions of mentoring/coaching programs provide a short-term snapshot, Daresh examines ELIS over 3 years, revealing important changes in the selection and preparation of mentors/coaches, expectations for their work with novices, and information that was collected to assess their influence on beginning principals' thinking and actions. For instance, in the second year of the project, data collection instruments were revised to determine how mentoring/coaching experiences influenced novices' competencies as defined by CPS: (1) develop and articulate a belief system, (2) engage and develop faculty, (3) assess classroom instruction, (4) facilitate and motivate change, and (5) balance management. Beginning principals and their mentors/coaches assessed how these competencies were developing over the year. In addition, year 3 saw significant changes, such as recruiting and selecting 20 full-time coaches rather than practicing principals, providing ongoing training and networking opportunities for coaches (e.g., learning blended coaching strategies), and establishing a rapid response team to address novices' concerns about managerial and technical issues (e.g., budgeting, contract management, scheduling).

Besides describing the evolution of the ELIS Project structures and processes, the chapter illuminates the impact mentors/coaches had on novices, a topic ignored in much of the literature on mentoring. The quality of mentoring and coaching activities improved as coaches used the CPS Principal Competencies to guide beginners' growth and they employed facilitative and collaborative blended coaching strategies, which novices also found useful in working with their own staffs. More attention was devoted to the annual school improvement planning process, allowing beginning principals to better understand the process, learn strategies to review previous years' student performance and achievement data, and establish realistic goals for school improvement.

As these six chapters have demonstrated, being a new principal or headteacher in the twenty-first century is full of trials and tribulations. It is critical for new principals and headteachers to receive support from the systems they work in as well as from their superiors. Without the requisite support, new principals and headteachers are likely to leave prematurely (Fuller & Young, 2009) and/or be unsuccessful in leading for learning. We hope readers not only gain new insights about the realities of beginning principals, but also stretch their thinking about ways of supporting novices as they take on the challenges associated with twenty-first century school leadership.

REFERENCES

Alsbury, T. L. (2009, May). *Translational leadership and the Innovation Leaders Academy.* Paper presented at the American Educational Research Association Annual Conference, San Diego, CA.

Alvy, H., & Coladarci, T. (1985). Problems of the novice principal. *Research in Rural Education, 3*(1), 39-47.

Fuller, E., & Young, M. D. (2009). *Tenure and retention of newly hired principals in Texas.* Dallas, TX: Texas High School Project Leadership Initiative.

Kowalski, T. J. (2009). Need to address evidence-based practice in educational administration. *Educational Administration Quarterly, 45,* 375-423.

Mazrui, A., & Kleban, T. (1986). *The Africans: A reader.* Westport, CT: Praeger.

National Association of Secondary School Principals. (2001). *Priorities and barriers in high school leadership: A survey of principals.* Reston, VA: Author.

CHAPTER 1

TRANSLATIONAL LEADERSHIP

New Principals and the Theory and Practice of School Leadership in the Twenty-First Century

**Bonnie C. Fusarelli, Matthew Militello,
Thomas L. Alsbury, Edwin Price, and Thomas P. Warren**

Educational leaders in the twenty-first century are expected to produce higher levels of learning for all students. To help future principals meet this challenge and successfully lead contemporary schools, many university-based preparation programs have redesigned their delivery formats, aligned their curricula to new professional standards, and updated their performance assessments for graduate students to more accurately reflect the new nature of leadership (Browne-Ferrigno, 2007; Jackson & Kelley, 2002; Murphy & Forsyth, 1999).

Over the last 2 decades, the role of the school leader has become more complex as the nature of the work has shifted. One reason for this shift is that schools have been in reform mode for several decades. Since the publication of *A Nation at Risk* (1983), the prevailing rhetoric has been that our schools are failing, and we must do something to fix them. Hence,

The Challenges for New Principals in the Twenty-First Century:
Developing Leadership Capabilities Through Professional Support, pp. 1–27
Copyright © 2010 by Information Age Publishing
All rights of reproduction in any form reserved.

apprentice models of school leadership preparation are no longer appropriate because they simply replicate the status quo. New school leaders must be prepared to be change agents, and therefore the nature of leadership preparation must change as well.

Over the last decade, the field of school administration has reframed itself and many administrator preparation departments have changed their names from Educational Administration to Educational Leadership. In much of the contemporary literature, the school administrator (principal) is now referred to as the school leader or school executive. This trend is more than a change in discourse or merely a matter of semantics, as it is intended to highlight a schematic shift in the way the role is conceptualized. Some critics might argue that the change is more cosmetic than substantive, but as this chapter will highlight, new ways of studying and preparing leaders have taken root in preparation programs and are reflected in the field's contemporary scholarship and practice.

In this chapter, we examine the evolution of school leadership in theory and in practice. We explore how school leadership has changed over time, and how these changes affect new (and existing) educational leaders. Drawing from data collected from a Q-sort research study and from a qualitative case study of one first-year principal, we illustrate how new school leaders are expected to be *translational leaders*. Translational leaders (Alsbury, 2009) cannot rely solely on a one-size-fits-all set of educational leadership practices but must apply relevant contextual diversity in their individual school community to generic standards-based practice. Principals translate the standards as they decide how to allocate their time and divide their energy within the school day. As we will illustrate, these decisions are often difficult because of conflicting demands on their time. This is particularly true for first-year principals who are uninitiated into the community of practice. They must find their "sea legs" while being jostled on the chaotic and often turbulent sea of modern school leadership.

THE CHANGING NATURE OF
NEW LEADER PREPARATION AND PRACTICE

To better understand the expectations for today's new school leaders, we begin with a brief history of the role of the school principal and how the expectations for that role have changed over time. Milstein (1993) divided the changing role of the principal into three distinct historical eras. During the first era, from approximately 1900 to 1954, school administrators acted as expert managers and embraced the values and practices of business and industry. The predominant view of school administration emphasized the principles of scientific management (Cooper & Boyd, 1987; Taylor, 1911). This corporate ideology continued to permeate school leadership, even as leaders adopted additional roles such as communicator, accountability expert, political strategist, and collaborator (Brunner, Grogan, & Björk, 2002).

During the second era (roughly 1950 to 1980) educational administration emerged as an established academic discipline (Culbertson, 1981). "Empiricism, predictability, and 'scientific' certainty' were emphasized" (Cooper & Boyd, 1987, p. 4). During this period, national organizations such as the National Conference of Professors of Educational Administration (NCPEA) and the University Council for Educational Administration (UCEA) were formed. By the late 1950s, the "theory movement" in educational administration was "firmly established and there was a determined effort to bring the social science disciplines (particularly psychology, sociology, and social psychology) to bear upon administrator preparation in education" (Crowson & McPherson, 1987, p. 47). This shift is readily identifiable in texts on educational administration, as Getzels (1977) noted, "None of the texts before 1950 referred to theory; virtually none of those after 1960 did not refer to it" (p. 10). One explanation for this shift was that theory was viewed as necessary for school leaders to utilize schools as vehicles for societal change.

The study and practice of administration, which had historically focused on relations within the school system, necessarily turned its focus outward to relations of the school system to other systems with which it was inextricably bound—political, legal, and economic systems, among others (Fusarelli & Fusarelli, 2005; Getzels, 1977). The generation, utilization, and study of theory led to the field of educational administration emerging as a legitimate academic discipline. However, emphasis on leadership development took a back seat or was secondary to theoretical inquiry into the nature of leadership.

By the 1970s, coursework in educational administration was thoroughly infused with behavioral science concepts and content, reflecting the belief that the practice of administration was "more than the execution of technical tasks" (Miklos, 1983, p. 159). Preparation programs focused on how education fit within the larger social system and how institutions and organizations affected the educational system (Miklos, 1983). School leaders were encouraged to view public education as an instrument of social policy. This paradigm became firmly entrenched in administrator preparation programs, but unfortunately, the social sciences were unable to solve the myriad problems confronting public schools.

The third era began in the 1980s. By the late 1980s, significant disparities in educational opportunities and outcomes became apparent and the inability of school leaders to solve these problems led to a series of attacks against education schools and the preparation of school leaders (Hess, 2004; Kramer, 1991; Levin, 2005; Tucker, 2003). University-based school leader preparation programs were criticized as being too theoretical and divorced from the actual practice of leadership. While some of these criticisms may have been warranted, it is important to note that the challenges of studying and teaching leadership in an applied discipline (such as education) are somewhat unique. For example, in political science the professor usually teaches *about* leadership. However, since they are preparing practitioners, professors in educational leadership programs are expected to teach their students how to *do* leadership, and do it well. There is a higher level of responsibility than in other disciplines to help students become effective leaders.

In an attempt to tie theory to practice and drive school improvement, in 1996, the Interstate School Leaders Licensure Consortium (ISLLC) adopted its "Standards for School Leaders." The adoption of the ISLLC Standards (or a modified version of the Standards) by over 43 states ushered in a fourth, standards-based leadership era in leadership preparation.

The 1996 ISLLC Standards represent a common core of knowledge, dispositions, and performances that link leadership and student achievement. The Standards focus on the centrality of student learning, the changing role of the school leader, the collaborative nature of school leadership, and encourage the use of performance-based systems of assessment and evaluation. They are anchored in the concepts of access, opportunity, and empowerment for all members of the school community.

The standards and accountability movement took hold and in 2001, the passage of the No Child Left Behind Act (NCLB) ushered in a fourth era of school leadership. NCLB requires standards and assessment for reading, math, and science to be set by each state and holds schools accountable for meeting these standards for all students. While standards for students and school leaders previously existed in many states, most did not have accountability measures attached—there were no consequences for failing to meet the standards. Today's school leaders are accountable for student success and tasked with promoting social justice and equity of educational opportunities for all students by creating a collaborative culture of adult and student learners (Grogan & Andrews, 2002; Lashway, 2002).

Within the past decade, particularly with the passage of the NCLB, principals have been called to lead systemic reform efforts and educate *all* children to proficiency, regardless of ethnicity, income, or family background. This shift in federal educational priorities, from equal opportunity to (near) equal outcomes, is dramatic and unprecedented (Fusarelli & Fusarelli, 2005). Simultaneously, how we train school leaders to meet these demands has come under heavy scrutiny (Hess & Kelly, 2007; Levin,

2005). For example, Levin (2005) posited, "The majority of programs range from inadequate to appalling, even at some of the country's leading universities" (p. 23). A number of studies of school leaders supported the Levin critique. In a study of school principals, Heller, Conway, and Jacobson's (1988) respondents indicated that graduate training was rigorous, but not necessarily valuable or aligned with the real world of educational leadership. Farkas, Johnson, and Duffet (2003) reported that 96% of practicing principals in their study cited on-the-job experiences and guidance from colleagues as more helpful in preparing them for their current position than graduate school. Most principals (67%) reported that "typical leadership programs in graduate schools of education are out of touch with the realities of what it takes to run today's school districts" (Farkas et al., 2003, p. 39). Hess and Kelly (2007) summarize:

> The vital question is whether the lack of attention to certain schools of thought regarding management may leave aspiring principals prepared for the traditional world of educational leadership but not for the challenges they will face in the 21st century. (p. 244)

However, there are signs that preparation programs are making the necessary changes. Militello, Gajda, and Bowers (2009) noted that principals reported taking more courses on the "use of data" and "accountability" since NCLB. Newer models of preparation have focused on pedagogy; organizational program features; a call for mentoring experiences; succession planning that is integrated into school improvement plans; and the proliferation of alternative certification programs (Alsbury & Hackmann, 2006; Pounder & Crow, 2005). Davis and colleagues (2005) reported specific characteristics of successful programs to include rigorous selection processes that address prior leadership experience; a clear program focus on and clarified values about leadership and learning; active, student-centered instruction; and supportive organizational structures to facilitate retention and engagement (Davis, Darling-Hammond, LaPointe, & Meyerson, 2005).

The profession has revisited and redeveloped its own standards as well. ISLLC re-authorized its standards in the fall of 2007 to reflect more recent research on the knowledge and skills necessary for successful school leaders. While many of the changes in leadership preparation originated from within the field in university-based preparation programs, responses to external pressures have driven much of the reform. Desperate to improve student achievement, policymakers in many states are revising licensing criteria and administrator certification requirements, shifting from input models (e.g., academic credits and certification) to output-driven models (e.g., competencies and performance) (Fusarelli, 2005).

Many states are passing seemingly contradictory reforms: either partially or totally eliminating barriers for entry of noneducators into school leadership (or allowing alternative pathways such as "add-on" licensure) while at the same time tightening regulations on university-based preparation programs through the adoption of state standards for school leaders and requirements for programs to be "approved" by outside accrediting agencies such as the National Council for the Accreditation of Colleges of Teacher Education (NCATE). In North Carolina, for example, the State Board of Education approved add-on licensure[1] and allows organizations other than institutions of higher education (IHEs) to recommend individuals for licensure. In 2009, the NC State Board of Education also mandated a "revisioning" of all university-based preparation programs requiring them to be centered on the seven new standards[2] for school executives: strategic, instructional, cultural, human resources, managerial, externally developed, and micropolitical. In *A New Vision for School Leadership*, the publication that introduced the NC Standards for School Executives, the authors noted that

> school executives of today must create systems for change and build relationships with and across staff … create a culture in which leadership is distributed and encouraged with teachers, which consists of open, honest communication, which is focused on the use of data, teamwork, research-based best practices, and which uses modern tools to drive ethical and principled, goal-oriented action. (North Carolina Department of Public Instruction, 2008)

Even so, some critics suggest an anathema between the ISLLC standards (and the various modified iterations of them) and school improvement. English (2005) noted, "The ISLLC standards are premised on a reduced role of the school administrator" (p. 97), implying a reciprocal expanding role for teachers. Murphy (2000) warned of the implications of reducing the complexity of the entire range of responsibilities of school leaders to a select number of standards. According to these opponents of standardization of educational leadership, there is requirement of return leadership preparation programs to strive for the inclusion of *human agency* (English, 2005, p. viii) into the study of educational leadership writ large. One primary premise behind this refocusing of educational leadership theory was to abandon the concept of standardization and focus on a more inclusive approach. English's (2005) "synoptic manifesto for change in educational leadership" (p. 27) suggests exploration into the interior and exterior view of each leader as they engage in their varying and decidedly nonstandard environmental contexts. It is with this paradigm shift in mind that we chose to use a new conceptualization of leadership theory known as *translational leadership* (Alsbury, 2009) briefly summarized below.

In summary, the role of school principals has changed and continues to be modified. External factors such as student accountability, increased public scrutiny of schools, and education leadership standards focus attention on the changing responsibilities of principals. Similarly, internal forces from within schools (a school's culture) shape and define the role of the principal. This contemporary education leadership landscape can be treacherous terrain, especially for a first-year principal.

TRANSLATIONAL LEADERSHIP

As discussed above, educational leadership theory has varied over time, moving primarily from a focus on scientific management to theories attempting to include the influence of diverse human relations within educational organizations. The current listing of leadership approaches or theories include instructional leadership, transactional leadership, and transformational leadership, to name a few. These theories of leadership practice have followed one another with one theory either refocusing on a different aspect of leadership or attempting to meld several previous theoretical foci.

In general, *instructional leadership* encourages the school to focus change goals on curriculum, instruction, teacher pedagogy, and student achievement measures. *Transformational leadership is* the practice of leading an organization through change; primarily through soliciting teachers to internalize a school's mission and willingly participate in a collaborative team that transforms the school culture and practice. Transformational leadership assumes that the central focus of leadership ought to be the commitments and capacities of organizational members (Leithwood, Jantzi, & Steinbach, 1999). Leithwood (1992) describes *transactional leadership* as leadership based on the exchange of services for rewards controlled by the leader. Educational leadership pundits have spent no small amount of effort attempting to compare and contrast instructional, transactional, and transformational leadership.

For example, Leithwood and colleagues (2000) suggest that instructional leadership leaves authority with the principal who is called to focus on managing the instructional program rather than their traditional attention on management tasks. Transformational leadership calls for the leader to focus the "commitments and capacities of organizational members" (Leithwood et al., 2000, p. 9). While transformational leadership focuses the leader on invoking higher levels of teacher commitment to organizational goals and creating a productive school culture, it does not provide a clear directive on who should maintain authority in the organization or that school leaders should focus on instructional improvement. In this respect, instructional leadership and transformational leadership have been criticized because the former provides a clear focus for administrative work but clarifies no specific process while the latter requires a specified process focused on developing faculty capacity but neglects to emphasize the instructional goals of schools. In addition, Leithwood (1992) suggests that transformational leadership evokes a more appropriate range of practice; it ought to subsume instructional leadership. Similarly, Sergiovanni (1990) argued that transactional leadership is a first stage in transformational leadership and central to getting day-to-day routines carried out. Day, Harris, and Hadfield (2001) suggest that we are entering an era of post-transformational leadership. It is their view that the failure of existing leadership theory to capture, explain, and represent current leadership practice lies in a reluctance to acknowledge that leadership is a complex, messy, and, at times, wholly nonrational activity that is value laden and value driven. Their findings indicate that morality, emotion, and social bonds provide far more powerful stimulants to motivation and commitment than the extrinsic concerns of other styles of leadership. This supports Burns' (1978) notion that the ultimate test of practical leadership is the realization of intended, real change that meets people's enduring needs.

Clearly there has been some disagreement among researchers pitting these leadership styles against each other. In fact, Marks and Printy (2003) suggested merging instructional and transformational leadership into an integrated style of leadership they termed *integrated leadership*. In our study, we embrace the notion that the human enterprise of education is too complex to adopt any of the current static theories of educational leadership and envisioned a new theoretical construct we call *translational leadership*.

"Translational leadership" (Alsbury, 2009) is a term adopted and modified from the medical field and applied to educational settings. Translational leadership was borne from, and is analogous to, a new approach for the translation of medical research to patient application known as translational medicine; a branch of medical research that attempts to more directly connect basic research to patient care. Translational medicine typically refers to the *translation* of basic research into real therapies for real patients. The emphasis is on the linkage between the laboratory and the patient's bedside, without a real disconnect. Translational medicine also focuses on the development and application of new technologies in a patient-driven environment—where the emphasis is on early patient testing and evaluation. Similarly, translational leadership is unique in its focus on leadership practices customized to the contextual realities of organizational variation in school districts attempting to implement and sustain innovation aimed at improving student achievement. Translational leadership focuses on localized cultural and organizational assessment and site-based action research defining the appropriate leadership approach for school administrators. Similar to the early contingency theories crafted by Blake and Mouton (1964) and Hersey and Blanchard (1977), translational leadership does not advocate a single leadership approach as superior, but encourages the development of custom-designed leadership emerging from an understanding of the unique needs and contexts of a local school or district. The use of a comprehensive and continual pattern of organizational assessment allows leaders to fine-tune their approach to match the natural lifecycle of all school cultures in the midst of innovative change.

Translational leadership then is the appropriate leadership style given the implementation of more authentic context-driven action research processes needed to design individualized action plans for school improvement. Translational leaders maintain a variety of effective leadership approaches, from directive to collaborative, and become adept at knowing how to collect the organizational data that helps them determine which approaches to use and when to use them. Adept translational leaders may in fact use several leadership styles within a single day, with each style requiring a different level of focus and time commitment. In this study, we investigate whether school principals do indeed use varied leadership approaches and focus on varied duties within different school contexts that occur between schools and within individual schools.

STANDARDS-BASED LEADERSHIP: Q-SORT DATA ON LEADERS' PERCEPTIONS

The changing demands on new school leaders are reflected in standards-based reform efforts. For example, principals in North Carolina are now required to learn and apply a new set of standards (see previous section). The North Carolina Standards for School Executives were developed through state-level revisions of the national Interstate School Leadership Licensure Consortium (ISLLC) standards. The ISLLC Standards claim to offer "blueprints of school leadership" (Murphy, 2003, p. 6) structured upon empirical findings about effective schools (Browne-Ferrigno & Fusarelli, 2005). The research foundation upon which the ISLLC standards were developed suggests that high levels of student academic achievement link directly back to school-leadership influences. Therefore, leaders who are trained in, licensed under, and evaluated on their effective implementation of the ISLLC Standards should link to improved student achievement. Yet, there is a lack of disciplined inquiry about the impact adoption of these new school-leadership blueprints have made (Browne-Ferrigno & Fusarelli, 2005).

In 2008, Alsbury, Militello, Fusarelli, and Warren (some of the authors of this chapter), conducted a study to determine how practicing school principals perceive and prioritize prescribed leadership standards, and how personal perception influences the enactment of preferred standards into their daily practice. The study focused on the Standards for School Executives in North Carolina and utilized Q-methodology to provide a framework for identifying diverse perspectives on a given topic (Brown, 1986). Q-methodology invites participants to make decisions about what is meaningful from their perspective on a given subject. Consequently, the method permitted the elicitation and examination of a set of viewpoints held by school principals regarding their practice of the North Carolina School Executive Standards.

In this study, our research question centered on how the North Carolina School Executive Standards are lived in practice by current school principals. As a result, we simply used the North Carolina School Executive Standards and the corresponding performance rubric. This rubric defined 33 "distinguished" performances within the seven overarching standards. For example, Standard 1, "Strategic Leadership," has four subgoals and each of these has a "distinguished" performance. The distinguished performance for Standard 1, subgoal B is: "The principals is a driving force behind major initiatives that help students acquire 21st twenty-first century skills." These distinguished performances make up the Q-sample for this study.[3]

Q-SORT FINDINGS

Three model sorts were found in this study, accounting for 40% of the variance (23.64 Eigen value). Forty-eight of the 61 participants (79%) loaded significant on one of these three factors. Each model sort provides insights into current principals' perspectives on their practice in relationship to the North Carolina School Executive Standards. Twenty-four of the participants (38%) significantly loaded on Factor A. This factor array is characterized with the school executive standards that highlight aspects of collaboration, empowerment, and facilitation. In fact, all of the standards sorted in the +3 and +4 columns have these words as primary descriptors or actions. As a result, we named this factor "*Distributing Leadership.*" Thirteen participants (21%) significantly loaded on Factor B. We named this factor "*The Challengers.*" The Executive Standards that loaded high in the distribution (+3 and +4 columns) connote visionary and challenging aspects of the principalship. Specifically, these principals target the development of a new vision of schooling as a primary aspect of their work. Eleven participants (18%) significantly loaded on Factor C. This factor is characterized by "vision." Here participants use their schools' vision to drive school improvement efforts as well as establishing a collaborative culture. As a result, we named this factor "*Leveraging Vision*." There is consensus and distinction (statistically significant) among a number of statements among the three factors. For instance, Standard 2.B.3 (informing district leadership) and Standard 6.B.2 (participates in developing district goals) both had extremely low z-scores in all three factor arrays (in the −3 or −4 columns in all arrays). Additionally, Standard 3.A.1 (establishes collaborative work environment) was in the +3 column in all three factors. It should be noted that the interview transcripts from the 61 participants in this study also informed our findings. These data were coded and analyzed and provided more insight into the participants' card placement decisions.

When we view how our first-year principals factored into this array we found more than half (6 of the 11) factored significantly on Factor A, and the remaining 5 on Factor C. These findings may indicate that newly minted school principals are more aware, if not prepared, to integrate elements of collaboration (Factor A) and using a vision (Factor C) to drive their leadership practice.

While the Q-sort provided important quantitative data on what key responsibilities principals spend their time on, it is also important to explore the detailed reasoning behind how and why principals make choices among equally important and sometimes competing duties. Therefore, we included the collection of qualitative data from each respondent through semistructured interviews of each principal. Due to space limitations we present a single case of one of the study participants.

A CASE STUDY OF A NEW PRINCIPAL IN PRACTICE

The Q-sort study described above focused on measuring leader perceptions and how their perceptions impact the usefulness of leadership standards. We know how these leaders perceive they concentrate their time, but we know little about the actual day-to-day challenges facing principals, especially new principals.

In the following section we present findings from a case study of a first year, middle school principal, Evan Cost.[4] Mr. Cost has been an educator for 17 years, 11 years as a high school English teacher and 4 years as an assistant principal in a middle school. He has worked in three school districts in North Carolina during his career. He is married and has three young children. When the principal of Central Middle School (CMS) was reassigned to become the principal of a newly open high school, Mr. Cost was appointed principal of Central Middle School. At the end of his first year as principal, Mr. Cost received the Administrator of the Year Award for his school district.

The fact that Mr. Cost won an award at the end of his first year of practice obviously makes him an outlier. However, we believe that it was the way he responded to the often very challenging situations he encountered his first year that set him apart—not the situations themselves.

In order to obtain a snapshot of a first-year principal's work environment and time management, Mr. Cost was asked to keep a detailed log of his daily activities for 3 week-long blocks (15 days). Mr. Cost recorded his activities and detailed what he did during each of the time blocks (see Appendix A). For the 3 weeks that his activities were logged, Mr. Cost worked an average of 63.5 hours a week.

North Carolina mandates that all school executives have a Professional Growth Plan (PGP). Mr. Cost's PGP had four main targets: (1) to make data accessible to teachers to impact instruction; (2) to utilize a collaborative leadership style; (3) to communicate to all customer groups; and (4) to continue at-risk programs. After each week of maintaining activity logs, Mr. Cost reflected on his week and then analyzed how he spent his time referencing both his own Professional Growth Plan, the North Carolina School Executive Standards, and Marzano, Waters, and McNulty's (2005) research on the 21 Responsibilities of the School Leader.

The first weekly log was recorded in late September. During that week, Mr. Cost worked a total of 63 hours. He spent approximately 3.5 hours (5%) of his workweek on student contact—2.5 hours of which were positive in the form of leadership activities and 1 hour of which was negative in the form of student discipline. Mr. Cost spent approximately 35 hours (55.5%) of his work week on teacher contacts—5 hours in general personnel issues, 15 hours conducting observations or being visible in the school, 2.5 hours in relationship building, and 12.5 hours doing duty (such as bus duty) with teachers. He spent 10 hours (15%) of his workweek on community contact—6 hours in meetings with various organizations and 4 hours in nondiscipline-related parent conferences. Mr. Cost spent another 10 hours on miscellaneous mandatory paperwork. He spent an hour (1.5%) in technology professional development on how to use Smart Board and another 3.5 hours (5%) on miscellaneous items.

In his reflection on his workweek, Mr. Cost noted that: "Upon accepting the position and evaluating the previous [school] administration, I resolved to make certain areas stronger at CMS. I wanted to be more of a *change agent*. According to Marzano, the change agent must protect those who take risks. I also wanted to develop better *communication* with the stakeholders. In order to do this, I wanted to be more accessible. Finally, I felt there needed to be an *order* developed at CMS. I proposed to reshape routine policies and procedures."

Later in the reflection, he highlights areas he perceived he needed to work on. Mr. Cost wrote:

> Using Marzano's research, my PGP, and my reflection of former administration, I have scrutinized my weekly log for September. I have determined from that week, I do not have enough teacher contact, and I am not involved with curricular issues as much as I need to be. I want to become more knowledgeable and involved with curriculum, and I must have more hours of teacher contact in my day.

He added action steps he could take to address his perceived needs:

> I have added weekly House/Department meetings for all five groups (6th, 7th, 8th EC, Exploration). I will attend one vertical meeting per month. I have changed the faculty meeting structure to allow for PLC group time (I participate in a PLC group during that time).

In early January, Mr. Cost completed a second weekly log. During that week, Mr. Cost worked a total of 60.5 hours (see Table 1.1). He spent approximately 23 hours (38% of his time) on teacher contacts (meetings, observations, etc.), 7 hours (12%) on student contact, 12 hours (20%) on communications with parents, 8 hours (15%) in professional development, and 9.5 hours (16%) on mandatory paperwork.

In mid-April, Mr. Cost completed a third weekly log. During that week, he worked a total of 66 hours (see Table 1.2). Mr. Cost spent approximately 33 hours (50% of his time) on teacher contacts (meetings, observations, etc.), 6 hours (10%) on student contact, 5.5 hours (9%) on communications with parents, 2 hours (5%) in professional development, 10 hours (20%) on mandatory paperwork, and 9.5 hours (6%) on miscellaneous items. It is interesting to note that according to his weekly time logs, by April his typical time to arrive at the school was almost 1 hour earlier than it was in September (5:00 AM instead of 6:00 AM).

The time logs and analysis of time spent detailed above give us a picture of how Mr. Cost spent his work days. He worked long days and still felt like there was never enough time to do everything he thought he should be doing. We believe his work schedule is fairly typical of first-year principals. However, Mr. Cost experienced many situations during his first year that would challenge even the most seasoned school leader.

At one of his first public events as principal, the middle school orientation meeting for students and parents, Mr. Cost had to call the police to break up a physical confrontation between two women. Apparently, the fight was initiated by a woman who did not like seeing her former hus-

Table 1.1.   Workweek Time Allocation: January

Category	School Day Hours (33)	% of School Day Hours	Total Work Hours (60.5)	% of Total Hours in Category	% of Each Category
Teacher Contact	19.5	60	23	38	
Staff Meeting	1.5	8	2.5		10
Personnel	0	0	2		9
Observation	13.5	69	14		61
Monitoring	4.5	23	4.5		20
Student Contact	1.5	4	7	12	
Positive	.5	33	.5		7
Negative	1	67	1		14
Duty	0	0	5.5		79
Parent Communication	10.5	31	12	20	
Professional Development	1.5	5	8	15	
Workshop	0	0	.5		25
Central Office Meeting.	1.5	10	6		75
Paperwork	0	0	9.5	16	

Table 1.2.   Workweek Time Allocation: April

Category	School Day Hours (33.5)	%	Total Work Hours (66)	% of Total Hours in Category	% of Each Category
Teacher Contact	23.5	70	33	50	
Staff Meeting	6.5	27	12	36	36
Personnel	1	4.2	1	3	3
Observation	6.5	27	6.5	19.6	19.6
Monitoring	9.5	41.8	13.5	41.4	41.4
Student Contact	3	9	6	10	
Parent Communication	2.5	8	5.5	9	
Professional Development	2	6	2	5	
Workshop	0	0	0	0	
Central Office Meeting	0	0	0	0	
Central Office Communication	2	100	2	100	100
Paperwork	0	0	10	20	
Miscellaneous	2.5	7	9.5	6	
School-Related Banquets	0	0	7	74	74
Visit Other School	.5	20	.5	5	5
Attend Funeral	2	80	2	21	21

band's girlfriend at their daughter's school orientation. While he was talking to the responding police officer, the school receptionist paged Mr. Cost over the public address system. When he arrived at the front office, he found the school secretary dialing 911 because a woman who had undergone surgery the day before was hemorrhaging and needed immediate medical attention. The orientation session got off to a bit of a rough start, but Mr. Cost used humor to defuse the situation when he addressed the group.

At the first school dance, a tornado touched down on the campus. Fortunately, even though tornados are exceptionally rare in the area (with only a handful on record), Mr. Cost and the other faculty heeded the weather center's storm warnings and had students take shelter in the brick corridors of the school. A tornado touched down on the school grounds, destroying several trees and causing minor damage to the school building. Although the students were shaken and upset, no one was injured. When the local television news noted that a tornado touched down in the vicinity of the school, panicked parents hastily arrived to pick up their children. Mr. Cost was able to manage the situation and avoid the chaos that could have ensued by following an emergency crisis plan that had been developed before the school year began.

The next external threat was from an armed bank robber who attempted to hide on the school's campus while attempting to evade the police. The police, pursuing the suspect, had their dispatch call the school and make them aware of the situation. Mr. Cost immediately put the school in lock-down. The police were able to capture the suspect, after which Mr. Cost immediately drafted a letter that was sent home with every child explaining what had occurred and why the school had been in lock down. He also employed the automated phone system and sent a voice message to each student's home phone number. There were two letters to the editor in the local newspaper the next week praising Mr. Cost's quick response to the threat and his quick communication with parents.

A few weeks later the school was in lock-down again, this time from an internal threat. A student brought a gun to school. He later reflected: "I stopped breathing for several seconds when I realized that there was a gun on campus." Again, his response was quick and averted a potential tragedy. He disarmed the student and immediately after the police left with the student in custody, he drafted a letter to parents that went home with every student that explained what had occurred. He also utilized the automated phone system again to leave a message with parents about what had occurred at school.

In addition to the challenges described above, Mr. Cost faced many challenges typical in school leadership, of which teachers being resistant to change was the most frustrating for him. In a humorous reflection on his first year as a principal, Mr. Cost came up with a list of things he learned during his first year. He presented the list at the last faculty meeting of the year. His reflections highlight just how challenging the first year as a principal can be. While some of the items reference the unique challenges he faced (e.g., ex-wives do not like to see their former husband's girlfriend at their daughter's school orientation; school dances should be scheduled only after looking at the Dopler; bank robbers do not mind hiding behind schools), many of the reflections illustrate the steep learning curve new principals face. Some of the most vexing problems for novice school leaders are those of relationship building and putting the theory into practice. That is, the translation of their preparation (and school leaders' standards) into actual practice.

Mr. Cost reflected on just how difficult it can be to effect change. He noted:

- "Inheriting a school that has had only two principals and has been very successful is not as easy as it first appears;
- Most teachers don't like change;
- I didn't know nearly what I thought I did at the beginning of the year;
- You make a first impression with the community, faculty, and staff only once;
- Perception is reality;
- Often, ideas from the top are not always practical;
- Teachers don't like change [he included this twice for emphasis];
- Change is inevitable;
- There will be many chances next year to comment on the changes by saying, "Well, I knew it wouldn't work and I told you so";
- Even when people disagree, they can come together;
- I have grown tremendously;
- Even though you may disagree with me, you will follow (maybe reluctantly) because you trust me;
- A great faculty and staff can compensate for a rookie administrator;
- I thank each and every one of you for helping me to grow this year!"

Other comments reflect challenges typical of any school disciplinarian. Mr. Cost's list of lessons learned included:

- "According to parents, school discipline is too strict, especially when it involves their child;

- According to parents, we have never communicated with them this year, especially if their child is performing poorly or misbehaving;
- Some parents are going to sue you if their child fails or if their child passes;
- In the last 2 weeks of school, parents ask what their child can do to pass."

These comments reflect the difficult task of balancing the needs of the school population with individual student needs.

Mr. Cost also noted some of the management issues most principals face. He commented that:

- "HR giveth and taketh away and without much explanation;
- Inventory that has never been done before can cause stress on many people in a building;
- Building HVAC can't keep up when it is 100 degrees ... well, not on the 8th-grade hallway anyway;
- Often principals' meetings can make you as angry as you have ever been ... until you realize that you do the same thing to the school faculty and staff;
- Mrs. Britt [the school secretary] was right when she said she had to train another principal;
- The building is so peaceful at 5:10 AM [the time Mr. Cost arrived at school by the end of the year];
- That Mrs. Wright [the previous principal] was right, you always get personnel surprises in May and June ... be ready."

In his reflections, Mr. Cost also commented on the heartbreaking challenges of working with disadvantaged student populations:

- "Sometimes no matter how many people help a kid, he will still "mess up";
- Students can walk off campus together, disappearing for 3 days and the people most stressed are school personnel."

He also noted some of the more personal challenges of being a school leader:

- "I am more OCD when under stress;
- Difficult times and stress only make us stronger ... and older, just ask my son Brian who wants to know why I am getting so old;

- I need lots of work when it comes to being sensitive;
- Not everyone has the same sense of humor ... in fact, some have none;
- We are a family and that is evidenced when something bad happens to one of us."

Finally, he concluded with a sentiment most beginning principals would agree with: "I am glad the year has come to a close, but the work ahead is overwhelming."

For the first-year principal, the "work ahead" can seem daunting. The professional path from novice to highly proficient school leader requires continuous reflection and learning from experience. It requires translational skills—taking theory and experience and weaving them into a tapestry of transformed, theory-based, and data-driven daily practice.

CONCLUSIONS AND IMPLICATIONS

This study dug into the practice of school leaders through the lenses of school leaders themselves. Such studies provide a realistic account of not only what is happening, but also what fosters and inhibits the leadership practices that improve teachers' practices and students' learning.

Our research confirms that most leaders prioritize and operationalize some, but not all, of the leadership standards. This is particularly true for new principals. Findings indicated a nearly even distribution between leaders who focused on distributing leadership (38%), visionary (21%), and a combination of leveraging vision to establish a collaborative culture (18%). The clear conclusion is that even when we standardize leader knowledge, performance, and disposition, leaders recreate their own customized mix of the standards to suit their own personal ideological and contextual needs. A key question not answered by this study is whether these leaders would have adopted the same set of leadership concepts to focus on even if a standardized listing were not provided. The outcome of this study does not necessarily support English's (2005) notion that a set of standards diminishes creativity of leadership foci, but does support his idea that leaders will tend to recreate their own personalized combination of leader standards to focus on. The caveat to this support is that leaders (new and experienced) tend to agree on a few key groupings of leader standards.

Other implications for the study findings include the promise of a methodological approach (Q-Sort) to help researchers identify ways leaders operationalize theoretical constructs. For instance, factor A helps us operationalize distributed leadership; that is, how leaders translate the concept of distributed leadership into their day-to-day behaviors. Finally, these results suggest that a preferable approach to leadership training is to provide a wide variety of leadership approaches. It should be remembered that study findings simply report what current leaders are doing, not necessarily what is most effective. It does, however, indicate why simply developing and teaching standardized lists to prospective principal candidates does not translate into implementation of these standards in the field.

These findings support the notion that Alsbury's (2009) construct of *translational leadership* best describes the actual operational practice of principals in the field. Namely, leaders assess their unique context day-to-day and even situation-by-situation and apply a customized blend of leadership style and leader standards. Further studies need to focus on how effective leaders spontaneously assess the changing context of their school environment, select from a variety of leadership styles and practices, and apply them successfully. This also suggests that leadership preparation programs should teach and assess aspiring leaders' ability to identify the elements of school culture and contextual variation, engage in ongoing and accurate internal assessment of the changing context, and apply a variety of flexible and appropriate leadership styles given the situation and context. This process of continual assessment-and-response reflects the true work of principals, distinguishes between effective and ineffective leaders, is largely ignored in current preparation programs, and belies the one-size-fits-all leadership styles.

We assert that the ever-increasing demands on twenty-first century school leaders will necessitate a new, fifth phase of leadership preparation and practice. Indeed, a new wave of more sophisticated understanding of leadership development is underway. The new wave is benefiting from a deeper appreciation that practical savvy must be connected to the application of theory. New school leaders can find their "sea legs" by becoming translational leaders; translating leadership standards and their theoretical knowledge as they decide how to allocate their time and divide their energy within the school day. Translational leaders will help steer their school toward improvement, even in the often turbulent sea of modern school leadership.

NOTES

1. Individuals with a master's degree in any field, can "add-on" administrator certification by completing an internship. In some cases the individual may be required to complete additional courses, but this is at the discretion of the endorsing institution.

2. The North Carolina Standards for School Executives are based on the 2007 ISLLC Standards.
3. The research instrument in Q-methodology consists of a set of opinion statements: the Q-sample (McKeown & Thomas, 1988). The goal of the Q-sample is to represent a given topic comprehensively. In Q-methodology, participants have the status of variables instead of sample items (McKeown & Thomas, 1988). Thus, Q-methodology does not require a large or randomly generated participant sample. The goal is to access deliberately a range of diverse, pertinent viewpoints on the investigated topic. In this study, 61 participants sorted card statements. The participants were a diverse group (based on demographic of gender, ethnicity, educational level, and school -level). Participants were asked to sort the 33 statements printed on 3" × by 1-inch" cards into a forced distribution ranging from "least characteristic of my practice" to "most characteristic of my practice." (See Appendix B.). Responses were recorded on an answer sheet grid depicting the forced distribution of nine columns with headings ranging from −4 (least characteristic statements) on the left side to +4 (most characteristic statements) on the right side of the spectrum.

    Participants were asked a series of questions regarding their decision-making processes after sorting the cards (e.g., "Describe why you selected the statement that you placed in the −4 column"). After the sorts were collected, they were analyzed using MQ Method 2.06 for Q-analysis (Schmolck & Atkinson, 1997). Keeping with common practice in Q methodology, principle component analysis was used to find associations among the different Q-sorts (Brown, 1980). In Q-methodology, it is the Q-sorts (or participants) that are factor-analyzed for intercorrelations, rather than the individual opinion statements. Q-sorts are the focus of analysis. Following factor analysis, emergent factors were rotated to simple structure (Varimax rotation). MQ Method produced defining statement "arrays" or model Q-sorts for each factor.
4. A pseudonym.

Appendix A: Diagram of Q-Sort

-4	-3	-2	-1	0	+1	+2	+3	+4

Appendix B: Example of an Abbreviated Weekly Log

Monday, September XX

6:00-7:10	Paperwork
7:10-7:35	Bus Duty
7:35-7:45	Hallways
7:45-7:50	Morning Announcements
7:50-8:05	Hallways
8:05-8:30	Beta Club Sponsors: Induction and Convention
8:30-9:00	Cafeteria Manager: Personnel Issue
9:00-10:00	Classrooms
10:00-10:30	SIP Meeting/PR Plan
10:30-11:00	Meeting with Church for Super Safe Schools Plan
11:00-11:30	Lunch with Cafeteria Staff
11:30-1:00	Cafeteria Duty
1:00-2:00	Classrooms
2:00-2:30	Return Phone Calls
2:30-2:45	Discipline
2:45-2:48	Afternoon Announcements
2:48-3:15	Transportation Duty
3:15-4:00	Peer Coaching Meeting
4:00-4:15	Recorded Crisis Connect Ed Messages
4:15-5:00	Paperwork
5:00-5:30	Worked on Planning Budget

Tuesday, September XX

6:00-7:00	E-mails
7:00-7:10	Worked on Power-Point for Guest Speaker at University
7:10-7:35	Bus Duty
7:35-7:45	Discipline
7:45-7:50	Morning Announcements
7:50-8:05	Hallways
8:05-8:30	Walking Campus Perimeter
8:30-10:00	Classrooms
10:00-10:30	Budget Meeting with Bookkeeper
10:30-11:00	Classrooms
11:00-11:15	Lunch
11:15-1:00	Cafeteria Duty

1:00-1:30	Discipline
1:30-2:00	Return Phone Calls
2:00-2:30	Meeting with Technology Facilitator
2:45-2:48	Afternoon Announcements
2:48-3:15	Transportation Duty
3:15-4:15	Smart Board Training
4:15-5:00	Paperwork
5:00-6:30	Athletic Booster Club Meeting

Wednesday, September XX

6:00-7:10	E-mails
7:10-7:35	See You at The Pole
7:35-7:45	Hallways
7:45-7:50	Morning Announcements
7:50-8:30	Parent Conference
8:30-9:00	Classrooms
9:00-10:00	Completed Planning Budget
10:00-11:00	Personnel: Cafeteria
11:00-11:15	Lunch
11:15-12:00	Cafeteria Duty
1:00-2:00	Discipline
1:00-1:30	Meeting with Bus Coordinator
1:30-2:30	Classrooms: Interviewed by Students in Global Connections
2:30-2:45	Prepared for SIP Team Meetings
2:45-2:48	Afternoon Announcements
2:48-3:15	Transportation Duty
3:15-4:15	SIP Team Meetings
5:00-6:30	PAPA Meeting

Thursday, September XX

6:00-7:10	E-mails
7:10-7:35	Gym Lobby Duty
7:35-7:45	Hallways
7:45-7:50	Morning Announcements
8:00-8:30	Senior Project Interview
8:30-9:00	Classrooms
9:00-10:00	Planning Budget
10:00-11:00	IEP

Appendix B continues on next page.

Appendix B: Continued

Thursday, September XX

11:00-11:15	Lunch
11:15-12:30	Cafeteria Duty
1:00-2:00	IEP
1:00-1:30	Discipline
1:30-2:30	Classrooms
2:30-2:45	Return Phone Calls
2:45-2:48	Afternoon Announcements
2:48-3:15	Transportation Duty
3:15-3:45	Paperwork
4:10-5:10	Power-Point Presentation for University Guest Speaker

Friday, September XX

6:00-7:10	E-mails/Paperwork
7:10-7:35	Gym Lobby Duty
7:35-7:45	Hallways
7:45-7:50	Morning Announcements
8:00-8:30	Men of Distinction Meeting
8:30-9:30	Classrooms
9:30-10:00	Parent Conference
10:00-11:00	IEP
11:00-11:15	Lunch
11:15-12:30	Parent Conference
12:30-1:00	Phone Calls about FB Game: Parents, Officials, Superintendent
1:00-1:30	Return Phone Calls
1:30-2:00	Meeting with 7th-Grade Teachers
2:00-2:30	Parent Conference
2:30-2:45	Paperwork
2:45-2:48	Afternoon Announcements
2:48-3:15	Transportation Duty
3:15-3:45	Meeting with Various Teachers
3:45-5:30	Paperwork
5:30-6:00	Dinner
6:00-9:30	School Dance

REFERENCES

Alsbury, T. L. (2009, May). *Translational leadership and the Innovation Leaders Academy*. Paper presented at the American Educational Research Association Annual Conference, San Diego, CA.

Alsbury, T. L., & Hackmann, D. L. (2006). The changing face of the profession: findings of the Iowa mentoring/induction program for novice principals and superintendents. *Planning and Changing, 37*(3/4), 169-189.

Blake, R. R., & Mouton, J. S. (1985). *The managerial grid*. Houston, TX: Gulf.

Brown, S. R. (1980). *Political subjectivity: Applications of q methodology in political science*. New Haven, CT: Yale University Press.

Brown, S. R. (1986). Q technique and method. In W. D. Berry & M. S. Lewis-Beck (Eds.), *New tools for social scientists* (pp. 57-76). Beverly Hills, CA: SAGE.

Browne-Ferrigno, T. (2007). Developing school leaders: Practitioner growth during an advanced leadership development program for principals and administrator-trained teachers. *Journal of Research on Leadership Education, 2*(3). Retrieved from http://www.ucea.org/JRLE/vol2_issue3_2007/BrowneFerrignoArticle.pdf

Browne-Ferrigno, T., & Fusarelli, B. C. J. (2005). The Kentucky principalship: model of school leadership reconfigured by ISLLC standards and reform policy implementation. *Leadership & Policy in Schools, 4*(2), 127-156.

Brunner, C. C., Grogan, M., & Bjork L. (2003). Shifting discourse defining the superintendency. In J. Murphy (Ed.), *The educational leadership challenge: Redefining leadership for the 21st century* (pp. 211-238). Chicago, IL: University of Chicago Press.

Burns, J. M. (1978). *Leadership*. New York, NY: Harper & Row.

Cooper, B. S., & Boyd, W. L. (1987). The evolution of training for school administrators. In J. Murphy & P. Hallinger (Eds.), *Approaches to administrative training in education* (pp. 3-27). Albany, NY: State University of New York Press.

Crowson, R. L., & McPherson, R. B. (1987). The legacy of the theory movement: learning from the new tradition. In J. Murphy & P. Hallinger (Eds.), *Approaches to administrative training in education* (pp. 45-64). Albany, NY: State University of New York Press.

Culbertson, J. (1981). International networking: Expanded vistas for leadership development. *Theory Into Practice, 20*(4), 278.

Davis, S., Darling-Hammond, L., LaPointe, M., & Meyerson, D. (2005). *School leadership study: Developing successful principals*. Stanford, CA: Stanford Educational Leadership Institute.

Day, C., Harris, A., & Hadfield, M. (2001). Challenging the orthodoxy of effective school leadership. *International Journal of Leadership in Education, 4*(1), 39-56.

English, F. W. (2005). Educational leadership for sale: social justice, the ISLLC standards, and the corporate assault on public schools. In T. Creighton, S. Harris, & J. C. Coleman (Eds.), *Crediting the past, challenging the present, creating the future* (pp. 83-106). Huntsville, TX: National Council of Professors of Educational Administration.

English, F. W., & Papa, R. (2009). *Restoring human agency to educational administration: Status and strategies*. Lancaster, PA: Proactive.

Farkas, S., Johnson, J., & Duffet, A. (2003). *Rolling up their sleeves: Superintendents and principals talk about what's needed to fix public schools*. New York, NY: Public Agenda.

Fusarelli, L. D. (2005). Gubernatorial reactions to No Child Left Behind: Politics, pressure, and education reform. *Peabody Journal of Education, 80*(2), 120-136.

Fusarelli, B. C., & Fusarelli, L. D. (2005). Reconceptualizing the superintendency: Superintendents as applied social scientists and social activists. In L. G. Bjork & T. J. Kowalski (Eds.), *The contemporary superintendent: Preparation, practice, and development* (pp. 187-206). Thousand Oaks, CA: Corwin Press.

Getzels, J. W. (1977). Educational administration twenty years later, 1954–1974. In L. L. Cunningham, W. G. Hack, & R. O. Nystrand (Eds.), *Educational administration: The developing decades* (pp. 3–24). Berkeley, CA: McCutchan.

Grogan, M., & Andrews, R. (2002). Defining preparation and professional development for the future. *Educational Administration Quarterly, 38*(2), 233-256.

Hess, F., & Kelly, A. P. (2007). Learning to lead: What gets taught in principal preparation programs. *Teachers College Record, 109*(1), 244-274.

Heller, R. W., Conway, J. A., & Jacobson, S. L. (1988). Here's your blunt critique of administrator preparation. *Executive Educator, 10*(9), 21-22.

Hersey, P., & Blanchard, K. (1977). *Management of organizational behavior: Utilizing human resources*. Englewood Cliffs, NJ: Prentice-Hall.

Hess, F. M. (2004). *Common sense school reform*. New York, NY: Palgrave Macmillan.

Jackson, B. L., & Kelley, C. (2002). Exceptional and innovative programs in educational leadership. *Educational Administration Quarterly, 38*(2), 192.

Kramer, R. (1991). *Ed school follies*. New York, NY: Free Press.

Lashway, L. (2002). The accountability challenge. *Principal, 81*(3), 14-16.

Leithwood, K. (1992). The move towards transformational leadership. *Educational Leadership, 49*(5), 8-12.

Leithwood, K., Jantzi, D., & Steinbach, R. (2000). *Changing leadership for changing times*. Philadelphia, PA: Open University.

Levin, A. (2005). *Educating school leaders*. Washington, DC: The Education School Project.

Marks, H., & Printy, S. (2003). Principal leadership and school performance: An integration of transformational and instructional leadership. *Educational Administration Quarterly, 39*(3), 370-397.

Marzano, R. J., Waters, T., & McNulty, B. A. (2005). *School leadership that works: From research to results*. Alexandria, VA: Association for Supervision and Curriculum Development.

McKeown, B., & Thomas, D. (1988). *Q methodology*. Newbury Park, CA: SAGE.

Miklos, E. (1983). Evolution in administrator preparation programs. *Educational Administration Quarterly, 19*(3), 153–177.

Militello, M., Gajda, R., & Bowers, A. (2009). The role of accountability policies and alternative certification on principals' perceptions of leadership preparation. *Journal of Research on Leadership Education, 4*(2), 30-66.

Milstein, M. (1993). *Changing the way we prepare educational leaders*. New York, NY: Teachers College Press.

Murphy, J. (2003). *Reculturing educational leadership: The ISLLC standards ten years out*. Fairfax, VA: National Policy Board for Educational Administration.

Murphy, J., & Forsyth, P. (1999). *Educational administration: A decade of reform.* Thousand Oaks, CA: Corwin Press.

Murphy, J., Yff, J., & Shipman, N. (2000). Implementation of the Interstate School Leaders Licensure Consortium Standards. *International Journal of Leadership in Education, 3*(1), 17-39.

National Commission on Excellence in Education. (1983). *A nation at risk: the imperative for educational reform: a report to the Nation and the Secretary of Education, United States Department of Education.* Washington, DC: Author.

North Carolina Department of Public Instruction. (2008). *North Carolina Standards for School Executives.* Retrieved from www.ncdpi.nc.us

Pounder, D., & Crow, G. (2005). Sustaining the pipeline of school administrators. *Educational Leadership, 62*(8), 56-60.

Schmolck, P., & Atkinson, J. (1997). *MQMethod (2.06).* Retrieved from http://www.qmethod.org

Sergiovanni, T. J. (1990). Adding value to leadership gets extraordinary results. *Educational Leadership, 47*(8), 23-27.

Taylor, F. W. (1911). *Shop management.* New York, NY: Harper & Row.

Tucker, P. D. (2003). The principalship: Renewed call for instructional leadership. In D. L. Duke, M. Grogan, P. D. Tucker, & W. F. Heinecke (Eds.), *Educational leadership in an age of accountability: The Virginia experience* (pp. 97-113). Albany, NY: State University of New York Press.

CHAPTER 2

NEW HEADTEACHERS IN SCHOOLS IN ENGLAND AND THEIR APPROACHES TO LEADERSHIP

Gillian Forrester and Helen M. Gunter

INTRODUCTION

The chapter presents the lived experience of being a new headteacher (principal) in England at a time when central control over the direction of education and what happens in publicly-funded schools has tightened considerably. Successive legislation over the last 2 decades has increased the micromanagement of activities so that schools, and those working within them, are subject to greater scrutiny and criticism. Simultaneously, the education service has been directed toward a market-based approach, where performance is transparent and standards and outputs are dominant. This provides more than a contextual backdrop for understanding professional practice, but enables the structuring impact of rapid and radical change to be understood through the exercise of agency within leadership as a social practice. We are particularly interested here in what

The Challenges for New Principals in the Twenty-First Century:
Developing Leadership Capabilities Through Professional Support, pp. 29–49
Copyright © 2010 by Information Age Publishing
All rights of reproduction in any form reserved.

it means for those new to headship (principalship): who they are, what they do, and how they understand their role. This chapter utilizes interviews with nine new headteachers, who at the time were within the first 5 years of headship appointments and working in either a primary or secondary school in different geographical locations in England. The interviews were conducted for the Economic and Social Research Council project, Knowledge Production in Educational Leadership (KPEL) (RES-000-23-1192) (Gunter & Forrester, 2008a). The chapter draws on this empirical research to discuss the leadership approaches taken and headteachers' perceived origins of their respective approaches.

THE CONTEXT

Publicly-funded schools in England have been subjected to a succession of educational reforms since the 1980s. The New Labour Government, which came into office in 1997, accelerated the pace of change and utilized education as a vehicle to realize a range of political ambitions linked primarily to developing a world-class education system. Policymakers sought to modernize a perceived underperforming education system and the failings of a poorly-led and managed teaching profession. Public funding for education increased substantially, but "significant improvements in standards" were expected by policymakers for the investment of "significant extra resources" (Department of Education and Employment, 1998, p. 4). The outcome for those working within schools has been incessant change and uncertainty resulting in an intensification of work, which is often performance data-driven; an emphasis on basic subjects, Standard Assessment Test scores, and performance targets, resulting in schoolchildren in England being the most tested in the developed world (Organization for Economic Co-operation and Development, 2008); high levels of bureaucracy, despite measures to reduce the administrative burden; inspection and auditing and greater monitoring and evaluation of activities; and numerous short-term initiatives and national strategies, which essentially regulate teachers' practice and methods. This restructuring, however, is not unique to England, but has featured across public services globally in a shift toward the New Public Management (Hood, 1995). Despite increased government intervention headteachers have overall responsibility of their school. As Southworth (2002) contends: "They continue to hold a formidable concentration of power and can exercise control over the form and direction of internal developments.... And, despite some cosmetic changes, power relations are (generally) remarkably enduring" (p. 196).

The New Labour government needed the support of headteachers to successfully implement policies and realize government's goals for education. Also, it was less complex to co-opt 24,000 headteachers as agents of reform delivery, rather than 400,000 teachers (Gunter & Forrester, 2010). This was achieved by investing in headteachers through different mechanisms, including running bespoke conferences to convey to headteachers the importance of modernizing education and their role within it; the selective use of specific forms of research evidence to explain a connection between headteachers and student outcomes; the establishment of a distinct college for school leaders, the National College for School Leadership (NCSL) for bespoke training programs, conferences, and research activities; the offer of financial incentives through higher pay and the award of honors (knighthoods and dames); and the inclusion of selected headteachers in policymaking processes as a means of securing political legitimacy.

The National Professional Qualification for Headteachers (NPQH), developed by the previous Conservative government, was designed for teachers aspiring to become headteachers. Formal preparation for headteachers was, however, considered to be patchy and disjointed (Daresh & Male, 2000; Gunter & Forrester, 2008b) and so New Labour reworked, updated, and designed new forms of training (National College for School Leadership, 2001). The NPQH remained, and there was the Headteacher Induction Programme (HIP) for new heads, and the Leadership Programme for Serving Headteachers (LPSH) for experienced headteachers. National Standards for Headteachers (Department for Education and Skills, 2004) were developed for training and accreditation purposes and essentially outline the competencies of effective headteachers and the requisites of headship (Gronn, 2003). The NCSL, launched in 2000, was the organizational unit used to house New Labour's framework for headteacher training and its official model of leadership (Gunter & Forrester 2009). The preferred model is "transformational leadership" (Leithwood, Jantzi, & Steinbach, 1999), which has been disseminated to headteachers via national training programs and standards. This model favors charismatic, "hero" heads whose personal attributes are influential on improving school outcomes. Transformational leadership requires visionary leaders who adapt their behavior in order to adhere to government imperatives for education. Subsequently a hybrid of transformational leadership has developed through the notion of distributed leadership where, through job redesign, effective delegation can be secured (Hartley, 2007). Qualified teacher status (QTS) is no longer a requirement for headship.

The socialization of heads is often characterized as "professional" and "organizational" (Crow, 2007; Hart, 1991). While acknowledging the professional socialization of school principals in the United States through university programs, Crow (2007) notes how:

> the organizational socialization of beginning principals is typically described as consisting of individual, informal, random, and variable learning.... Beginning principals essentially make sense of their roles by themselves or by using informal feedback from teachers, students, parents, and other administrators. (p. 312)

A longitudinal study (Earley & Weindling 2004; Weindling & Earley, 1987) suggests that "most of the groundwork is put in place during the first five years or so" (Weindling & Dimmock, 2006) and the following main problems encountered by new heads are identified:

- Style and practice of the previous head
- Rundown school buildings
- Communication and consultation with staff
- Public image of the school
- Weak members of the senior team
- Incompetent staff
- Low staff morale

Hobson and colleagues' (2003) findings are similar and noted additional issues new headteachers confront, including "feelings of professional isolation and loneliness, managing the school budget, and implementing new government initiatives" (p. ii). Holligan, Menter, Hutchings, and Walker's (2006) study of the needs and priorities of new heads elicited "an extremely diverse picture, suggesting that there are many factors contributing to the formation and nature of headship" (p. 103). How headteachers approach their leadership work is likely to change due to inevitable changing circumstances and as they become more experienced in the role. The career trajectories of headteachers has been conceptualized by some researchers as comprising a series of stages or phases (e.g., Earley & Weindling, 2004; Gronn, 1999). This research, however, may entail headteachers contemplating retrospectively when they can reflect upon the resonance of their leadership over a period of years as well as rationalizing any transitions. Heads at the beginning of their leadership pathway present a more embryonic account of their leadership approach and Gronn's (1999) four-stage leadership career framework encompasses a second stage of accession, or the preparation and positioning to be a leader. This work is important as it explains how heads make the shift to locations of influence in their school and elsewhere. Research evidence suggests that the contexts in which headteachers are working varies enormously and Gunter (2001) has called for leadership "to be conceptualised in ways that provide an understanding of the dynamics" (p. 84). The research reported below attempts to address this need.

THE RESEARCH

Sample

The KPEL project investigated the origins and development of school leadership in England (Gunter & Forrester 2008a). Twenty-five head-teachers were involved in the project and, of these, nine had recently attained the NPQH and had successfully been appointed as headteachers. This chapter focuses specifically on the data generated through interviews with those nine new headteachers; some biographical details are presented in Table 2.1 along with some descriptive characteristics of each headteacher's school.

The nine headteachers comprising the sample share the relative newness of the school leader role and may have had similar recent leadership preparation and formal training. However, they work in different types of school settings and contexts; some are heads in small primary schools in rural locations, others are leading large secondary schools in towns or cities. The institutions may be faith schools (denominational), nondenominational, comprehensive community schools, or specialist schools. The performance of the school, as defined by its league table positioning, may be low- or high-performing or somewhere in between. The composition of the pupils differs as do the numbers of teaching and support staff and the school leadership team. The new headteachers have had different career trajectories and professional experiences; their own perspectives and philosophies about education and learning; and different expectations, attributes, and personal resources. The nature of leadership therefore needs to be understood within a historical, social, and cultural environment, which invariably affects and determines a headteacher's approach.

Procedures

The sample of 25 headteachers was purposive. Following the approach of Ribbins and Marland (1994), we "tried to select people who we believed would be interesting [and were] different in terms of their life experiences and their views" (p. 7). First, colleagues in higher education institutions—whom we knew had dealings with headteachers through their academic

Table 2.1. Sample of New Headteachers in the KPEL Project

Headteacher	Sex	Years as Headteacher	Headships	School Phase, Type, and Size	School Location
Naomi	Female	5	1	Secondary; comprehensive, nondenominational; 910 pupils, mixed, 11–16 years	Urban; an area of broadly average social disadvantage; pupils eligible for free school meals (FSM)—above national average
Jane	Female	4	1	Secondary; comprehensive, voluntary controlled; 950 pupils, mixed, 11–16 years	Urban; an area of above average social disadvantage; pupils eligible for FSM—is broadly average
David	Male	3	2*	Secondary; comprehensive, nondenominational; 1,010 pupils, mixed, 11–16 years	Urban; an area which is near the bottom of all socioeconomic indicators
Lisa	Female	3	1	Secondary; comprehensive, nondenominational; 750 pupils, mixed, 11–18 years	Urban; a less prosperous area of the locality; pupils eligible for FSM—above national average
Mary	Female	3	1*	Primary; denominational; 70 pupils, mixed, 4–11 years	Rural; in an area with broadly average economic circumstances; pupils eligible for FSM—below national average
Cheryl	Female	3	1	Primary; denominational; 190 pupils, mixed, 4–11 years	Urban; in an area with little disadvantage; pupils eligible for FSM—below national average
John	Male	2	1	Primary; denominational; 200 pupils, mixed, 3–11 years	Urban; in an area with much disadvantage; pupils eligible for FSM—well above national average
James	Male	2	1	Primary; denominational; 255 pupils, mixed, 3–11 years	Urban; in an area where socioeconomic circumstances are below average; pupils eligible for FSM—above national average
Martin	Male	1	1	Primary; denominational; 160 pupils, mixed, 4–11 years	Rural; in an area with little disadvantage; pupils eligible for FSM—well below national average

*About to move to another school/headship post

activities, for example, through Continued Professional Development (CPD) and postgraduate work, school partnerships, or membership of professional associations—were asked to recommend suitable participants. Also during our interviews with other project participants (e.g., policymakers, education leadership researchers), interviewees were invited to suggest the names of people whom they considered we should speak with; the names of some headteachers were offered in this way. Second, it was important for the research that the sample included participants who had become headteachers when it was not necessary to receive the NPQH training, as well as those who had come to headship more recently and had thus obtained the NPQH. A list of headteachers who had been through the various NCSL training programs (NPQH, HIP, LPSH, etc.) was therefore obtained from the NCSL following our request to suggest 40 names at random of headteachers who might be approached for interview. Third, it was important to ensure a pluralistic sample in relation to gender, age, and ethnicity as well as having coverage of credentials, organization, attributes, and choices, as outlined in Figure 2.1.

A larger sample of 25 headteachers was constructed so that there were substitutes already identified in case personal and/or professional events prevented someone from taking part. A letter and the project description were mailed out inviting participation. Prior to each interview a short factual questionnaire was dispatched in advance of the visit to obtain biographical information and relevant details about the school. Headteachers were each interviewed once; the duration of each interview was typically 1 hour and 30 minutes. The relationship between the nine headteachers and the total sample of 25 is one of recentness and experience. The research approach was biographical and the headteachers were invited to narrate how they came to leadership and who they were influenced by, how they understand their role and work, and how they would ideally prefer to undertake it. Specifically, the term "approach" was utilized because we were interested in the "doing of leadership" and how these heads "do" leadership. A framework of questions focused on the following:

1. Reasons for becoming a headteacher
2. Nature of their training and professional development
3. Likes and concerns about headship
4. Views of New Labour's policies for education
5. Their understanding of official model(s) of school leadership
6. Leadership approach and how it takes place
7. How their leadership approach had been learned
8. Perceived effectiveness of their leadership approach

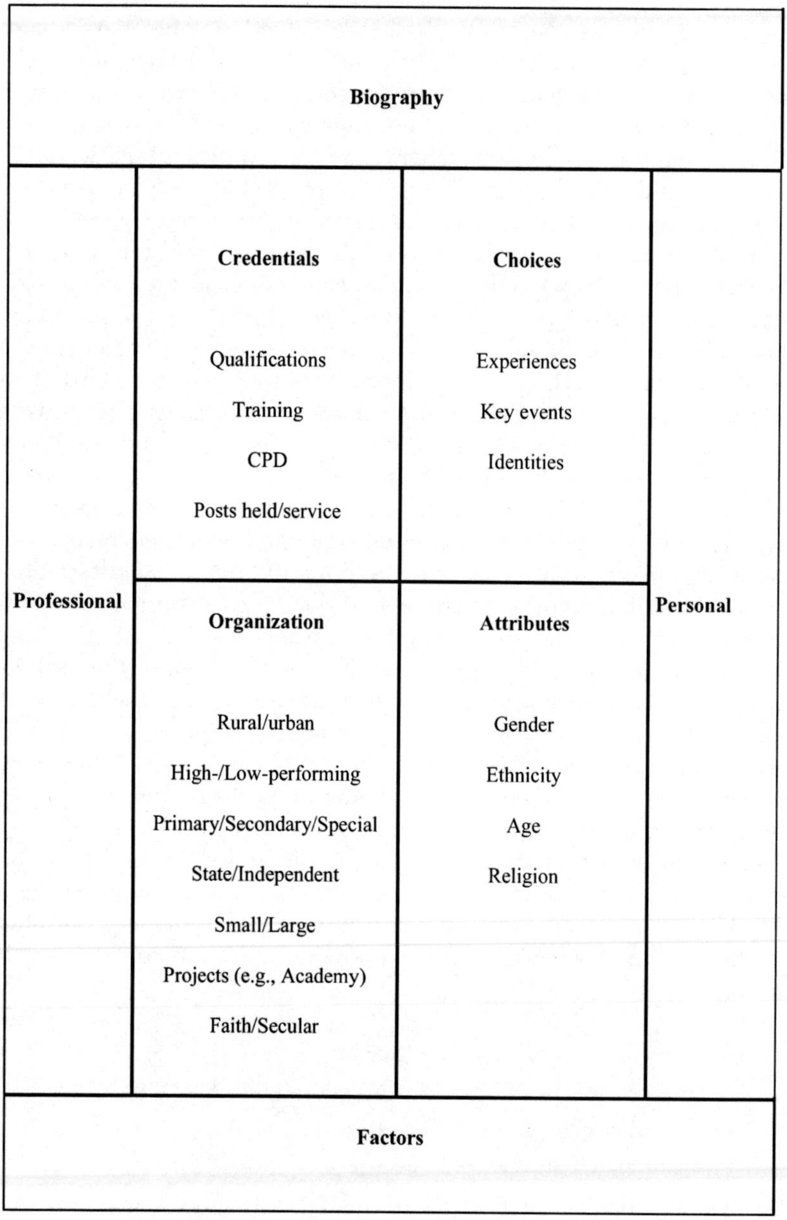

Biography			
Professional	**Credentials** Qualifications Training CPD Posts held/service	**Choices** Experiences Key events Identities	**Personal**
	Organization Rural/urban High-/Low-performing Primary/Secondary/Special State/Independent Small/Large Projects (e.g., Academy) Faith/Secular	**Attributes** Gender Ethnicity Age Religion	
Factors			

Figure 2.1.   Headteacher sampling framework.

The following section reports mainly on findings from guiding questions 6 and 7 and data is also used from questions 2 and 4 to exemplify specific points.

LEADERSHIP APPROACHES

Being Visionary

One of the salient features in the data is headteachers' articulation of a "vision" for their respective school and their ambitions to facilitate school improvement:

> If you haven't got a vision or a strategic view of where you can see your school in the next 5 years, and what you're hoping to achieve at that school, and for the children, then there's not a lot of point in being a school leader. (Martin)

Having organizational vision, a sense of mission, as well as inspiring and shaping staff members' attitudes, values, and beliefs are features of transformational leadership; "vision" is increasingly regarded as an imperative for effective leadership. The extent to which the new heads acquiesced to the notion and transformational leadership varied. For example, James did not appear to have any comprehension of a New Labour model for school leadership. In response to the question regarding government advocating a particular model of leadership, he responded:

> I'm not sure that I know what it is ... I've got my own principles that I believe are sound ones and those are things that inform what we do. (James)

James's stance contrasts sharply with that of John who stated he was inclined to "lean toward" the transformational model of leadership. Of the nine new headteachers, John appeared to be most engaged with the NCSL through courses, networks, and training:

> I'm reasonably satisfied with the model I'm getting because ... I enjoy those areas of support and personal development that are part of that package ... on a spectrum of 1 to 100 I would go 85 with the model that's been given to me. (John)

Doing Leadership

The new headteachers do, to varying degrees, talk mostly about their leadership approach as being collaborative, shared, dispersed, and open and that they delegate. These features are important components of their individual approaches. Mary's approach, for example, typifies the notion of a shared leadership:

> This is a small school and I would like to think it is shared leadership really as much as possible. And I have a very open style...everything that goes on we discuss in a very open way. Ultimately I have responsibility, I know that, and in a bigger school you would have the different layers of leadership that you could cascade down, but here we are small staffed so we discuss it ourselves. (Mary)

Mary divulged, however, that she was taking up another headship elsewhere shortly where she intended to be "different." The smallness of her current school necessitated her working with staff "very much at ground level," but that meant there was "no distance" and, with hindsight, she aspired to be more "assertive" in her next post. Naomi considered that her approach was collaborative and staff consulted on and discussed together big issues:

> We've made a huge amount of major changes; all of the big things have been based on a lot of consultation with the staff...the key to change being successful is that everybody has felt in the end that it has been a joint decision. (Naomi)

David and Jane both expressed their approaches in terms of having different phases. Initially it was necessary to dictate what needed to be done, though after changes had been made their approach to leadership altered. David explained how due to the pressures of an imminent Ofsted inspection and the school being about to fall into the category of special measures he had to "really crack the whip and get stuff done." He rationalized:

> When I first took up the headship, it was very didactic, it was very direct, very coercive, it was very, you know, "this is how it's going to be done, you've got to do it this way." (David)

However, after the school had undergone some "massive transformations" David perceived his approach to be "a much softer sort of leadership ... I've dispersed leadership much, much more." Jane's experience was similar. She described her initial approach as "very directive" because she perceived what needed to be done and she "had to get the staff confidence." Now, and after 4 years in the post, Jane is "giving people as much ownership as I can." She elaborated:

> It's collaborative now, but it wasn't initially because I didn't have the time for it to be.... It was very much when I came in, "this is what I want for the school. This is my vision for the school; there you are, look at it. Right, is there anything there you can't sign up to?" And it was that kind of approach. (Jane)

Making Changes, Making a Difference

New headteachers will, potentially, be enthusiastic with a quest for identifying priorities and actualizing school improvement, while also be seeking a smooth transition of integration within the school and forging their own identities. How the new heads in this study initially proceeded in their leadership approach ranged from undertaking early and dramatic changes (as evidenced by the examples of David and Jane, above), or moving cautiously, or perhaps delaying initial changes that were hampered by obstinate systems or staff. Resistance to change from staff was encountered by some new heads on a number of levels; some members of the staff team, for example, preferred or were used to the ways of the previous headteacher. Handling the legacy of the previous headteacher was a focal issue in the data. Some of the new heads were replacing a retiring headteacher who had been at their school for a considerable number of years. John recounted how "the previous incumbent in this position...was here for 28 years." He divulged:

> Under my predecessor the parents dominated ... their social baggage dominated the school.... When [name of previous head] was here ... there would be a lot of emotion in the school and there would be threats and screaming and shouting (from the parents) and she would placate them like a mother.... Initially in the first few months I had some of that but then I think the signal went out that "he doesn't do personal and social baggage."(John)

John considered that it was partly due to him being a male headteacher that he was able to take a different approach than the previous head. John's approach was to "empower" parents rather than "cater to their emotions." In John's case, parents were a socializing source in the school through the particular challenges they presented.

James succeeded a head that had been at the school for 20 years. He perceived that changes to the school needed to be made quickly as "this school was in a fairly poor state of affairs." He found himself "having to

drive things along initially" and because he had "some really, really difficult staffing issues," it was necessary to remove one person due to "gross
misconduct." This required him "to make some hard and fast decisions."
However, he talked about having to "absorb some of the culture as well"
and so blending his own aspirations for the school with existing practices
encompassed his approach in the early stages of his headship. He was
mindful that "actions speak louder than words" and "people learn about
what you believe by the sorts of things that you do and how you do
things."

Cheryl, spoke of the difficulties of succeeding a head who had spent his
whole professional career at the school (37 years), of having to now work
with the deputy who had applied for the headship post she had herself
obtained, and of a long-serving teaching staff who had served under the
previous head for many years. The first year of Cheryl's headship thus
involved her maintaining a balance between directing and facilitating
what she perceived as necessary changes to school systems, structures,
staffing, and buildings, while also gaining the support, confidence, and
commitment from staff (and governors, parents, pupils) for her vision for
the school. Martin articulated similar challenges:

> Change has been very difficult to orchestrate here, because I am a different
> leader to the previous head. (Martin)

Clearly, for these heads, the first few years of formation and accession
is a period of adjustment, making mistakes and learning from them, modifying their leadership approach, ascertaining their strengths and
weaknesses and that of staff, building a committed team around them,
and articulating and gaining commitment for a particular vision. Their
leadership approaches were influenced by the local context and circumstances, changing external demands, composition and personalities of
staff, and personal attributes of the head. The following section reports
on how the new headteachers believe their leadership approach has been
learned.

ORIGINS OF LEADERSHIP APPROACH

> What's molded my leadership ... has been the experiences, role models,
> and the NCSL and the HIP. And without those, I wouldn't be the leader I
> am at the moment. (Martin)

The new headteachers have learned to lead and continue to learn how
"to do" leadership from a combination of different sources. The research
investigated the preparation for the role, who and what had been most

influential, and where the new heads perceive their approaches originate. Role models, postgraduate study, and national training programs were identified as significant factors and these are now examined in turn.

Role Models

The professional learning of leadership is ongoing throughout a head-teacher's career. Arguably, a view of headship probably begins with one's own experiences of being a pupil/student and is then formulated through working under particular types of headteachers as teachers, heads of department, deputy headteachers, and assistant heads. The headteachers could identify particular leaders whom they have encountered in their teaching career who have been role models and/or mentors. Clearly, their observations of others, both "good heads and bad heads" (David), are extremely influential in the shaping and development of their own ideas regarding the kind of leaders they themselves are striving to become. For example:

> The most important thing is role models ... I can see bits in me of other people that have been there throughout my time in teaching ... I can think of five headteachers who were all very different; very different style but very effective within their schools.... That is the biggest influence absolutely ... I can think of people that I didn't respect, and I don't ever want to be that kind of leader. (Jane)

> I've worked with a lot of good people over the years ... middle managers as heads of years, or other deputies, or other heads. And I've consciously watched people in action and consciously looked at how people handle diffi-cult situations. And so I think that has shaped the way that I go about the job. (Naomi)

New heads appear to model their own approach to leadership on the practices of those leaders whom, for a variety of reasons, they admire. In this sense they are socialized into the occupational norms of the role and so fashion their leadership skills and capabilities in accordance with what they perceive as an appropriate or effective approach to leadership. Simi-larly, they have perceptions regarding poor leadership and so negative role models are also influential in terms of how not to be.

Postgraduate Study and National Training Programs

Various learning opportunities have been available to the new heads through their career trajectories, leading up to preparation for headship and beyond. Four headteachers, for example, have undertaken master's degree courses (MA, MEd, MSc) offered by higher education institutions. The NPQH, introduced in 1997, became a mandatory requirement from April 2009 for those taking up first headships. This has been detrimental to the uptake of master's courses in higher education institutions that teachers might once have undertaken for career advancement purposes. As Jane explained:

> I resisted NPQH massively when it first came out ... and I thought "I have just nearly killed myself doing a part-time MA," which I was doing as well as working full time and it did nearly kill me. And suddenly that's not being recognized because of the decision to do my MA was around into moving into leadership and moving within my career.... I needed to learn more about leadership in order to be able to do it. But I had done this and I have learned a lot and I have read a lot, and suddenly along came NPQH; "Hey, you can't get into headship without that!" (Jane)

> I probably wouldn't have done a master's degree had NPQH been around in 1990, because that would have been the automatic qualification before. You always got a master's degree before. (David)

It is not possible to determine to what extent postgraduate study affected the actions of the new heads. It seemed that for many heads in the total sample a master's qualification was a means to an end in terms of professional development. Now the NPQH was the step to take for teachers seeking promotion. However, in comparison, a few of the longer-serving headteachers truly valued their postgraduate studies, and two had gone on to study for PhDs. Unlike the longer serving headteachers participating in the KPEL project, all the new heads had received formal preparation for headship through undertaking training for the professional qualification of the NPQH via the NCSL. All nine new heads appeared to find the training useful in terms of leadership preparation and were generally quite favorable toward it, for example:

> I think doing NPQH, in fact, gave me a greater ambition in terms of being a head. I think it also gave me the confidence to know that I could do it. (John)

> The NPQH, some of the sort of discussions about the philosophy of leadership and the differences between leadership and management, you know they helped crystallize my own ideas. And you know that was very useful to talk from an academic perspective about being a headteacher really. There was very little in it that which was to do with day-to-day issues. (James)

> I found the master's very stilted ... a lot of it really didn't impact on the day job and even when I became a deputy I didn't really draw on, there was a

few parts that I did, the understanding of different learning styles and the way that you work with people … [the NPQH was] all very hands-on and real and relevant to the job. Although I don't think the NPQH makes you a good headteacher, I think it's probably the most relevant experience you can have that can help you prepare for headship. (Lisa)

Lisa articulated her opinions on the value of NPQH, and while she seemed satisfied with the program she voiced concerns about the current nature of the headship role, which was, in her opinion, deterring many capable teachers from becoming headteachers:

People are making conscientious decisions now to do with the expectation of a head in the 21st century and I think that is putting people off…. I know from one of the colleagues who has since left us, when she was studying her NPQH she said a lot of people were saying, "I want to get a deputy headship, but I don't want to go any further." (Lisa)

In terms of other national programs, five had taken up funding opportunities (£2,500 grant) to undertake the HIP (now Early Headship Provision), and two others were midway through it. One had also completed the LPSH (now Head for the Future program). These programs appear to have assisted in maintaining heads' engagement with the NCSL for the duration of the program after which they might become disengaged from NCSL. In terms of the relationship the nine heads had with the NCSL at the time of the interviews, an analysis of the data revealed that four heads could be described as engaged with the college (e.g., attended conferences and courses, actively involved in NCSL-related networks), two had partial engagement (due to requirements of HIP training), and three were disengaged (no direct contact).

Knowledge Utilization

Headteachers, arguably, can draw upon particular forms of knowledge, texts, and research that subsequently inform and shape their thinking and practice. One of the striking features in the data was that, given the volume of research around school leadership nationally and internationally and a proliferation of leadership texts, dedicated journals, and bespoke research reports, the heads in the KPEL project actually made very little use of this kind of literature. The new heads often had good intentions to read more and indeed effective leadership books have been purchased by some and similar reading material downloaded and saved from the NCSL websites for future perusal. Interestingly, literature that heads were particularly drawn toward appears to be of a particular nature (known and named authors were typically Fullan, Gardner, or Goleman). The explanation usually given for lack of opportunities to read was insufficient time, exacting demands of the role, and the sheer volume of memoranda, directives, and initiatives awaiting and requiring their attention, such as "policies, statements, governor's things, government things ... the Specialist Schools stuff" (David). Indeed, a number of heads had very large (unread) piles of these kinds of documents and paperwork in their offices. Largely due to the intensity of school leadership work, there is little if any space in the day-to-day running of schools to reflect on and critique one's leadership practice. More importantly, there is little professional space to properly contemplate any alternatives to what they are doing or opportunities to question and indeed challenge the means by which they are being asked to transform and improve schools in the ways now thoroughly embedded in the system by policymakers/government.

DISCUSSION

The difficulties identified by new headteachers as they take up the role are not dissimilar to those already indicated in previous studies (Hobson et al., 2003; Holligan et al., 2006; Weindling & Dimmock, 2006). The socialization of heads in a reform context is intense and complex (Crow, 2007). An outcome of the KPEL project research was the creation of a dynamic positioning of leadership approaches (directive, directed, distributive, and inclusive), which heads might embrace at different times and under different circumstances (Forrester & Gunter, 2009). Positions are not exclusively fixed and, at any time, more than one might be appropriate. The *Directive* Approach is a position taken by heads when they have a strong sense of their own purpose as the leading professional (i.e., headteacher). The *Directed* Approach is similar, but the direction and the process by which change is taking place may be under the direction of other interest groups, for example, internally via school governing body and/or externally via school inspectors. There are times when both approaches are overlain with the language and behaviors of the official New Labour model of heroic heads as transformational leaders, where the heads present themselves as charismatic, inspirational, and visionary. For the Directive Approach, this can mean when the headteacher adopts the New Labour persona as one congenial to him- or herself in driving forward their agenda, while for the Directed Approach this can mean adopting an approved identity in order to deliver. The *Distributed* Approach follows official good practice; headteachers are directed toward creating diverse workforce roles and delegate the responsibility and accountability for tasks and projects. The *Inclusive* Approach incorporates the notion of the school community. Professional and personal relationships are crucial, as are mutual exchanges, understanding, and trust.

This dynamic positioning of approaches helps to explain the complexity of leadership approaches. From the headteachers' accounts, it is apparent, for example, that Mary has unsuccessfully inhabited the Inclusive position and is aspiring to be more Directive. Jane and David, while they have both been in dialogue with Directive and Directed, are now shifting their positions more toward Inclusive. John also appears to be in dialogue with Directive and Directed; he has a strong sense of leadership identity and is actively determining school purposes, but this is in tension with being directed via NCSL training. As the new heads in this study experience their first headship (or, in David's case, second) there is usually a tendency to be Directive initially with a move later toward being more Inclusive. The KPEL project findings suggest that the model of school leadership in policy is not necessarily the same as the one in play by headteachers themselves, where it appears to be more a product of experience than formal training, is highly situated in the history and locality of the school, and depends on personal labor (intellectual and emotional), attributes, beliefs, and values of the individual heads (Forrester & Gunter, 2009; Gunter & Forrester, 2010).

Data from the experienced (6–15 years, $n = 9$) and veteran (over 16 years, $n = 7$) headteachers in the sample offer a useful contrast of perspective to those more recently appointed (Forrester & Gunter, 2009). The longer-serving heads in the study appear to realize that it has been necessary, for a variety of reasons, to change their approach and indeed expect to change. Some expressed their headship careers in phases/stages along with reasoned explanations for transitions, as has been found in other research about headship (Earley & Weindling, 2004). Interestingly, the veteran heads articulate the greatest sense of educational values (Ribbins, 2004), whereas the recently appointed and most of the experienced position themselves with policy implementation, although usually with an emphasis on making initiatives work at the local level. Despite official prescription and the pervasiveness of government reforms, which restrict school leaders' freedom and professional autonomy (Gronn, 2003), there is evidence in the data to suggest some experienced and veteran heads are operating or have operated under the radar; as long as their school is producing favorable results, they find they have some space for maneuver and can use their own agency.

The new headteachers consider that they learned their approaches from other leaders who have acted as role models or mentors and through received wisdom and to a lesser extent courses and training, as found by Daresh and Male (2000), despite the massive investment in leadership training through the NCSL since that research was undertaken. It seems that headteachers have little time for reading and looking at research evidence. This raises the question that if leading and leadership is learned rather than trained, then surely there are implications for the substance of national training programs; Hobson et al. (2003) suggest that support provision should be flexible, individualized, and negotiable. However, new headteachers' socialization is not straightforward or necessarily the same; certainly it is not a case they have arrived at their schools with a "tabula rasa." The new heads, however, were generally more accepting of the restructuring of education and compliant with central decisions and strategies than their experienced and veteran counterparts. Nevertheless, there was also evidence of some resistance when reforms were perceived as incommensurate with their local context. Human agency is evidently at play as the data reveals how the new heads reconcile their leadership work with their own educational values and existing professional perspectives. Indeed, the new heads in this study are responding to increasing complexity and intensity of the role (Crow, 2007). The push for improved "performance" seems to cause some friction between government and individual heads' priorities about education and educating. Conflicting priorities clearly raises concerns about the nature of school leaders' work, how it will be judged, and what is professionally expected of them (Ribbins, 2004).

Coming in with sometimes considerably different ideas than their predecessors, their own vision for the school, and, for the majority of the new headteachers, a focus on improving the school, the new head could be viewed by staff as perhaps bringing some relief to low morale and new opportunities, and/or be seen as challenging existing practice and the school culture. This period of headteacher changeover (Hart, 1991) seemed a particularly intensive time for those new heads in smaller primary schools and the larger secondary schools. Primary heads typically have a much smaller teaching staff compared to their secondary counterparts and so the head and staff in primaries are more likely to be in closer proximity whereby they work as a team of 5–15 teachers, with perhaps a leadership team comprising two or three people. This is compared to secondary heads that may have many separate subject departments, a teaching staff of perhaps between 50 and 80 people, and also a leadership team comprising between 5 and 10 people. However, those new heads in larger secondary schools appeared to have more difficulties within the context of existing formal and informal structures and mechanisms, greater staffing and personnel issues, and gaining commitment from others for their own vision for the school. The experiences of primary and secondary heads are thus different in terms of the numbers of people they are required to lead and manage and the structures in which they work. It is therefore more practical for secondary heads to respond to the invitation of distributing leadership simply because the job as it now stands is too big for one single person to effectively manage.

CONCLUSIONS

This research offers meaningful stories from those working on the front line of education and who are charged with implementing school reforms. Illuminating the lived realities of leaders and leading within their localized complexity is, in our opinion, more important than seeking to identify the traits and attributes of effective leaders. The KPEL project is distinctive as it has explored headteachers' leadership approaches within a framework incorporating the state, public policymaking, and knowledge production/ utilization in the construction and configuration of school leadership in England. The training of school leaders was viewed by policymakers as vitally important, as was the qualification for headship (NPQH) along with a visible, physical structure in the form of a college; the building is particularly significant and representative of the importance of leadership and headship. (Although if the Conservative party gains office in government in 2010, the indications are that the NCSL will be axed.) The new headteachers in the study are thus, to some extent, a product of the formalized development activities of the NCSL programs. Yet while their participation in programs clearly has some impact upon shaping the leadership practices of some heads, new headteachers typically utilize individual agency in the formation of their leadership identity as leaders. The KPEL research has indicated that headteachers encounter similar problems in the early years of their headship. However, other influences such as geographical and socioeconomic locality of the school, legacy of their predecessor, a school's size and type, and the head's personal attributes and experiences appear to have a more significant contribution to headteachers' socialization and development (Crow, 2007). While the KPEL project has investigated these issues in some detail, further study is required, and perhaps with a larger sample of heads that is longitudinal, ethnographic, and involves biographical methods of investigation, so that leadership approaches can be mapped against the appropriate dynamic positioning over a period of years.

Professional development activities must therefore respond to a host of local contextual issues, and these issues seem particularly poignant for heads of smaller primary schools and larger secondary schools. The NCSL currently monopolizes research and training of school leaders, indeed arguably postgraduate preparation for leadership has been hijacked by the needs of policy implementation. Future research should address the impact and effectiveness of different professional development opportunities and how heads reconcile national programs with their own conceptions of leadership as well as investigating in more depth if and how postgraduate study (master's, EdD, PhD) undertaken in universities has affected their leadership approaches.

This chapter has explored the new headteachers' experiences of leading schools in a complex and unstable educational environment. The contemporary headteacher role was revealed as they talked about encountering stressful challenges, tackling new responsibilities, risk taking, making mistakes, and unanticipated crises, as well as how they are gaining confidence, honing their identities as school leaders, developing survival skills, and having opportunities for some direct influence on educational processes. The heads bring to their schools a unique and multifaceted set of personal attributes and resources. These heads are at the beginning of their leadership pathways and so their accounts offer an emergent picture of leadership approaches in schools in England in the early twenty-first century.

REFERENCES

Crow, G.M. (2007). The professional and organizational socialisation of new English headteachers in school reform contexts. *Educational Management Administration and Leadership, 35,* 51–71.

Daresh, J., & Male, T. (2000). Crossing the border into leadership: Experiences of newly British headteachers and American principals. *Educational Management and Administration, 28,* 89–101.

Department for Education and Employment (DfEE). (1998). *Teachers: Meeting the challenge of change.* London: The Stationary Office.

Department for Education and Skills (DfES). (2004). *National standards for headteachers.* London: Department for Education and Skills.

Earley, P., & Weindling, D. (2004). *Understanding school leadership.* London: Chapman.

Forrester, G., & Gunter, H. M. (2009). School leaders: Meeting the challenge of change. In C. Chapman & H. M. Gunter (Eds.), *Radical reforms: Public policy and a decade of educational reform* (pp. 67–79). London: Routledge.

Gronn, P. (1999). *The making of educational leaders.* London: Cassell.

Gronn, P. (2003). *The new work of educational leaders: Changing leadership practice in an era of school reform.* London: Sage.

Gunter, H. M. (2001). *Leaders and leadership in education.* London: Chapman.

Gunter, H. M., & Forrester, G. (2008a). *Knowledge production in educational leadership project.* Final Report to the Economic and Social Research Council (ESRC) RES-000-23-1192.

Gunter, H. M., & Forrester, G. (2008b). New Labour and school leadership 1997–2007. *British Journal of Educational Studies, 56,* 144–162.

Gunter, H. M., & Forrester, G. (2009). Institutionalised governance: The case of the National College for School Leadership. *International Journal of Public Administration, 32,* 349–369.

Gunter, H. M., & Forrester, G. (2010). Education reform and school leadership. In S. Brookes & K. Grint (Eds.), *The new public leadership challenge.* London: Palgrave.

Hart, A. W. (1991). Leadership succession and socialization. *Review of Educational Research, 61,* 451–474.

Hartley, D. (2007). The emergence of distributed leadership in education: Why now? *British Journal of Educational Studies, 55,* 202–214.

Hobson, A., Brown, E., Ashby, P., Keys, W., Sharp, C., & Benefield, P. (2003). *Issues for early headship – Problems and support strategies. Summary report.* Nottingham, UK: National College for School Leadership.

Holligan, C., Menter, I., Hutchings, M., & Walker, M. (2006). Becoming a head teacher: The perspectives of new head teachers in twenty-first-century England. *Journal of In-service Education, 32,* 103–122.

Hood, C. (1995). Contemporary public management: A new global paradigm? *Public Policy and Administration, 10,* 104–117.

Leithwood, K., Jantzi, D., & Steinbach, R. (1999). *Changing leadership for changing times.* Buckingham, UK: Open University Press.

National College for School Leadership. (2001). *Leadership development framework.* Nottingham, UK: Author.

Organization for Economic Co-operation and Development. (2008). *Education at a glance: OECD Indicators.* Paris: Organization for Economic Co-operation and Development.

Ribbins, P. (2004). Context and praxis in the study of school leadership: A case of three? In H. Tomlinson (Ed.), *Educational management. Major themes* (Vol. 3, pp. 131–146). Abingdon, UK: Routledge Falmer.

Ribbins, P., & Marland, M. (1994). *Headship matters. Conversations with seven secondary school headteachers.* Harlow, UK: Longman.

Southworth, G. (2002). School leadership in English schools. In A. Walker & C. Dimmock (Eds.), *School leadership and administration. Adopting a cultural perspective* (pp. 187–204). London: Routledge Falmer.

Weindling, D., & Dimmock, C. (2006). Sitting in the "hot seat": New headteachers in the UK. *Journal of Educational Administration, 44,* 326–340.

Weindling, D., & Early, P. (1987). *Secondary headship: The first years.* Windsor, UK: NFER-Nelson.

CHAPTER 3

SO YOU WANT TO
BE A HEADTEACHER?

"Liabilities of Newness," Challenges, and
Strategies of New Headteachers in Uganda

**Pamela R. Hallam, Julie M. Hite,
Steven J. Hite, and Christopher B. Mugimu**

The higher a chimpanzee stands, the more its naked bottom is exposed.

My mentor provided the above proverb to put over the point that you cannot avoid people critiquing you when you are a top administrator, so you need to create an atmosphere where people feel free to critique you, because once they know that they have that freedom they will eventually become more as contributors to your growth than as people that are working toward your downfall. (Samuel)

This remarkable advice was the response of a seasoned Ugandan school leader when a new headteacher asked how to survive the emotionally intense early years of his administration. Not unlike their U.S. counterparts, new Ugandan headteachers are "bombarded with all the responsibilities that a veteran principal has ... which creates burnout, stress, and

The Challenges for New Principals in the Twenty-First Century:
Developing Leadership Capabilities Through Professional Support, pp. 51–76
Copyright © 2010 by Information Age Publishing
All rights of reproduction in any form reserved.

ineffective performance" (Crow, 2006, p. 46). They often work in resource-poor schools that lack basic supplies and equipment, and no specialized training is required or provided for them. They are assigned based on past teaching performance or on their relationship with influential members of the school's founding body. Their dilemma is complicated by the fact that in Uganda, many students come from distressed circumstances, which include extreme poverty, medical deprivation (including HIV/AIDS), poor housing conditions, and single-parent homes.

The qualitative research reported in this chapter examines the challenges of new school leaders in developing countries, with the goal of informing and improving headteacher preparation. The review of literature addresses the role of leadership in school performance, reviews challenges of new principals in developed countries, and provides the context of the Ugandan education system. Findings highlight challenges and coping strategies of new Ugandan headteachers, and the discussion addresses theoretical and practical implications for improving performance of these new school leaders and their schools.

LITERATURE REVIEW

This effort is grounded in strategic leadership at the confluence of leadership, organizational, and strategic theories. This nexus posits that leadership affects organizational performance (e.g., Davies & Davies, 2006; Scott & Davis, 2007). The style and strategy of leaders affect the motivation of organization members (Ballinger & Schoorman, 2007), as well as the organization's mission, culture, design, control systems, networks, and ability to adapt to its external environment (e.g., Hanna, 2001; Lunenburg & Irby, 2005). From this perspective, schools are organizations seeking successful performance for student learning, and school leaders such as principals or headteachers have a critical role in a school's successful performance.

Theoretical Framework

A general consensus among researchers acknowledges leadership as a key factor when a school outperforms others with similar students (e.g., Hite & De Grauwe, 2009; United Nations Educational, Scientific and Cultural Organization [UNESCO], 2009). While most of the principals' influence on student outcomes is indirect, principals do make a difference in student achievement (e.g., Cotton, 2003; Hallinger & Heck, 1996;

Marzano, Waters, & McNulty, 2005). Cotton (2003) indicated that "while … principals' direct interactions with students in or out of the classroom may be motivating, inspiring, instructive, or otherwise influential, most of it is indirect, that is, mediated through teachers and others" (p. 58). Principals positively affect student achievement by influencing those with more direct interactions with students, primarily their teachers. Reviewing the literature, Leithwood, Seashore-Louis, Anderson and Wahlstrom (2004) concluded that "leadership is second only to classroom instruction among school-related factors that influence student outcomes" (p. 5).

Yet a new school leader may not be adept, capable, or effective in supporting strong school performance. In the literature on organizational theory, the term *liability of newness* is often applied to new organizations (Baum, 1996; Stinchcombe, 1965). Liabilities of newness suggest that a new organization experiences disadvantages due to (1) costs of learning new roles, (2) costs of developing new organizational systems, and (3) underdeveloped social relationships that result in insufficient social capital and trust (see Figure 3.1).

Learning new roles, developing and redesigning the school's organizational systems, and developing relationships to build critical social capital require time. As a result, new leaders may struggle to sustain school survival and generate academic performance. Understanding more about such challenges of new leaders may be of value in developing effective leadership strategies that support school performance.

New School Leaders

School leaders in developed nations. Research on new school leaders, which has focused on developed nations, has found that new principals

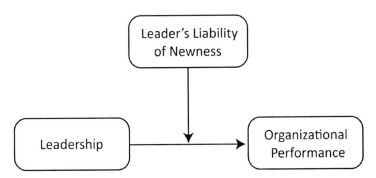

Figure 3.1.   Liability of newness as an influence on leadership and organizational performance.

struggle with clarifying their roles, enacting instructional leadership, adjusting to the profession and the individual school system, and feeling stressed over their new role (Daresh & Playko, 1992, 1994). New school leaders also wrestle with professional isolation, government initiatives, school management, preexisting legacies, school budgets, and ineffective staff (Hobson et al., 2003). To facilitate the preparation of these new leaders, some form of licensure is generally required, which includes a university degree, administrative internship, and appropriate exams (LeTendre & Roberts, 2005). Yet even with this preparation, these new principals still struggle with liabilities that come with being new to the job. Like leaders of other organizations (as cited above), they must adapt to their new roles, learn to understand and manage their school's systems, and develop critical networks for the school.

School leaders in Africa. A comprehensive online search of English-language scholarly journals, as well as the online databases of UNESCO and World Bank, reveals that little primary research has addressed issues facing new school leaders in developing countries in Africa. While studies of school leadership in South Africa dominate numerically, the range of other African countries in the leadership research literature is represented by Botswana, Kenya, Malawi, Namibia, Tanzania, Togo, Uganda, and Zimbabwe (Hallam, Hite, Hite, & Mugimu, 2009). The liabilities of newness and resulting challenges for new leaders in these educational contexts may differ from those in developed countries, given scarce resources, a prevalence of schools without government support, and few if any preparation requirements. Therefore, strategies and solutions cannot simply be prescribed for all groups of new school leaders regardless of national or regional location (Kitavi & van der Westhuizen, 1997; Memon & Bana, 2005). The study at the heart of this chapter exemplifies how new school leaders in developing countries, specifically Uganda, may more effectively advance school performance.

Education in Uganda

Uganda is located in equatorial eastern Africa on the northwestern shore of Lake Victoria. The capital city of Kampala has a population of approximately 1.4 million. Excluding Kampala, the 25 largest cities range in population from about 37,000 (Hoima) to 160,000 (Kira). Supporting a population of 32.7 million (nearly equal to Canada), the land mass of Uganda is roughly the size of Great Britain. The country is divided into four administrative regions and approximately 80 districts. Mukono District, the location of this study, is situated directly east of Kampala District and has a population of nearly 800,000. Since the political turmoil of the

Idi Amin years (1971–1979), Uganda has achieved a reasonably stable and peaceful political condition.

According to UNESCO (2009), the most recent data show 7,364,000 students enrolled in Ugandan primary schools (approximately 100% enrollment rate), 760,000 students at the secondary level (16% enrollment rate), and only 88,000 at colleges or universities (3% enrollment rate). Female students comprised 50% of the primary school population, 44% of secondary, and 38% of tertiary students.

The Ugandan education system. In the 1890s European Christian missionaries introduced the first formal schools in Uganda, and by the early 1900s there were a few government-operated schools as well. By the late 1950s and early 1960s government and private schools were operating across the country.

Having descended from the British educational model, Ugandan schools are designed to prepare students to pass rigorous compulsory national examinations. Seven years of primary education culminate in the national Primary Leaving Examination (PLE). Students can then move on to the first 4 years of secondary education—the "O" (Ordinary) level, after which they sit for the Uganda Certificate of Education (UCE) examination. Based on their UCE performance, they may qualify for 2 final years of secondary education, the "A" (Advanced) level. The Uganda Advanced Certificate of Education (UACE) examination completes the A-level schooling cycle for Ugandan students, and their UACE scores determine whether they may continue on to postsecondary study.

Primary and secondary schools in Uganda are operated by the government, church organizations, nongovernment organizations, and private interests. Due to severe limitations in funding and other critical resources (Hite et al., 2006), schools fully funded by the government are not prevalent in Uganda. Most primary and secondary schools are privately operated, funded by school fees and personal investments from the school director and board of directors, though many receive partial government support. Many schools began with support by religious groups, but few are actually governed or funded by church affiliation. Private secondary schools range from first-year startup enterprises in rural and urban areas, with as few as 20 students, up to multicampus school systems with 6,000–8,000 students. Thus there is significant market pressure, competition for tuition-paying students, and instability in the rates of survival for new and emerging private schools. As entrepreneurial entities, these schools must acquire resources from the environment (Hite & Hesterly, 2001), mostly from school fees.

The current market saturation of private secondary schools allows students and families to choose schools that can enhance their future educational opportunities (Hite et al., 2006). Schools that are unable to attract enough fee-paying students, manage the school's scarce resources, and prepare students to pass examinations often fail. These competitive pressures are evident in the Mukono District of Uganda, where the rate of failure for secondary schools between 2003 and 2008 was nearly 30% (Hite, Hite, Rew, Mugimu, & Jacob, 2009). The responsibility for success in this competitive context falls almost entirely to the headteachers, many of whom are inadequately prepared for these significant challenges.

Administrative organization of Ugandan schools. As illustrated in Figure 3.2, the Ugandan Ministry of Education and Sports (MOES) administers government schools, and the founding body or board of directors (BOD) governs private schools. The BOD, by law composed of three or more school owners, provides vision and direction for the school. Ownership equity distribution varies among schools, and one director is likely to own a majority share and have greater influence. The BOD hires the headteacher, who acts as school site supervisor for the day-to-day operations and serves as the financial controller. All government and most private schools also operate with a board of governors (BOG), an official body that ensures that the interests and policies of the MOES are followed. The BOG is composed of a chairperson who is the headteacher at a same-level school (i.e., secondary), a teacher representative, a community leader, a politician, an official from the district education office, and parent representatives. The BOG assists the headteacher in making day-to-day decisions in the school and in dealing with teacher-related discipline issues. The BOG is most influential in government schools; in private schools the BOD tends to exert more influence.

The headteacher supervises the deputy headteacher and the director/ dean of studies (DOS). Most schools have two deputy headteachers: one over academics, who supervises and works closely with the DOS to supervise teaching and students' assessment, and one over administration, who ensures quality of services provided to students and community.

Traditionally, Ugandan headteachers are promoted from the school where they teach (Hite et al., 2009). Often the school director promotes a teacher into the position of deputy headteacher or director of studies and then to headteacher. Sometimes a teacher goes directly from the classroom into the position of headteacher without any administrative experience whatsoever. By either route, the new headteacher has no formal leadership training at college or university to help in surviving the challenges of the first critical years of administration. This process is similar to ascension dynamics in Pakistan (Memon & Bana, 2005) and the Bahamas (Tooms, 2007), where teachers are promoted to positions of school leadership based solely on teaching ability, without administrative training.

This research seeks to understand the challenges of new school leaders in developing countries and some of the ways they meet these challenges,

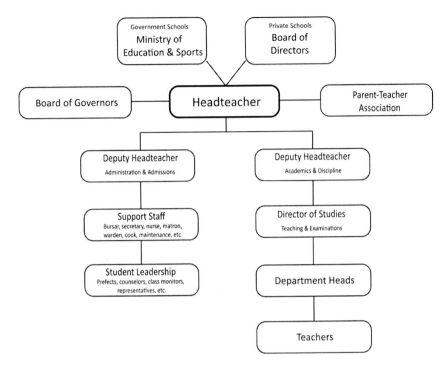

Figure 3.2.   Typical administrative structure of Ugandan schools.

with a specific focus on Uganda. The results and conclusions inform those in positions to support new headteachers, such as the Ugandan Ministry of Education, universities, and school directors. Of special interest are the challenges and potential strategies and their implications for selecting and training new leaders to implement national education goals and sustain school performance. The following questions have guided this research:

- What are the challenges faced by new headteachers in Uganda?
- What are the strategies and sources of help to which new Ugandan headteachers turn in addressing these challenges?

METHODS

Within the theoretical framework of strategic leadership, this research investigated how new leadership can affect school performance, and how liabilities of newness (Baum, 1996; Stinchcombe, 1965) may challenge this process. Theoretical understanding of new school leaders in developing countries is limited. Thus the purpose of this research was to describe and explain headteachers' lived experiences in the transition to this new leadership role, using a grounded theory approach (Glaser & Strauss, 1967; Strauss & Corbin, 1998). Themes and patterns of the challenges and strategies that emerged from the data are presented.

Sampling

A two-stage, purposeful, stratified sampling process identified headteachers from 20 schools. For maximum variation, the 224 secondary schools in Mukono District, Uganda, were grouped in four categories based on two criteria: (1) whether government-aided or private; and (2) whether large or small (fewer than 300 students). The main inclusion criterion for schools in the study population was having a "new" headteacher, defined as a headteacher meeting at least one of the following three criteria: (1) having fewer than 4 years' total experience as a headteacher (60%), (2) serving in his or her first headteacher assignment (75%), or (3) having recently transferred from one headteacher assignment to another at a different school (25%). Most headteachers from government schools were new to the school (75%), whereas most headteachers at private schools were brand new (93%).

The first sampling strategy included two schools in each category. The second attempted to represent the proportion of school types, as new headmasters may function in any of them. For example, the district had a majority of private schools (87%), most of which were small (97%). This distribution is reflected in 75% of the new headteachers sampled being from private schools, and a majority of small schools being included. As 16% of headteachers in the district were female, this study included 20% new female headteachers. The final sample was moderated by headteacher availability and willingness to participate. Table 3.1 provides the sampling distribution. Table 3.2 lists informants by pseudonym, gender, and school demographics.

Table 3.1.   Stratified Sampling of Schools and Headteachers (*n* = 20)

	Govt (*n* = 5)	Private (*n* = 15)	Total
Large (*n* = 9)	3	6	9
Small (*n* = 11)	2	9	11
Total	5	15	20

Table 3.2.   Sample of New Headteachers

#	Pseudonym (Name)	Gender	Experience			School	
			Newness	Yrs at School	Yrs as Headteacher	Governance	Size
1	David	Male	New to School	3	11	Govt	Large
2	Steven	Male	Brand New	7	7	Private	Small
3	Paul	Male	Brand New	1	5	Govt	Small
4	Daniel	Male	Brand New	2	2	Private	Large
5	John	Male	Brand New	3	3	Private	Small
6	James	Male	Brand New	2	2	Private	Small
7	Thomas	Male	New to School	1	3	Govt	Large
8	Edward	Male	Brand New	1	1	Private	Small
9	Caroline	Female	Brand New	6	6	Private	Small
10	Susan	Female	Brand New	3	3	Private	Large
11	Robert	Male	Brand New	1	1	Private	Small
12	Joshua	Male	New to School	7	11	Govt	Large
13	Jacob	Male	Brand New	2	2	Private	Large
14	Charles	Male	New to School	5	9	Private	Small
15	Matthew	Male	Brand New	2	2	Private	Small
16	Rachel	Female	Brand New	2	2	Govt	Small
17	Peter	Male	Brand New	1	1	Private	Small
18	Samuel	Male	Brand New	4	4	Private	Large
19	Isaac	Male	Brand New	6	6	Private	Large
20	Margaret	Female	Brand New	2	2	Private	Large

Data Collection

Data collection centered on 60 to 90-minute semi-structured interviews of new headteachers in the Mukono District, Uganda. Interview questions asked informants to describe the challenges they had experienced or were experiencing in their positions and their strategies for addressing these challenges. Interviews were recorded and transcribed to facilitate further data analysis, and informants were assigned pseudonyms (see Table 3.2).

Data Analysis

Qualitative analysis of the data followed an inductive and constant comparative strategy (Glaser & Strauss, 1967), facilitated by NVivo software. Within the framework of grounded theory, the analysis facilitated "developing theory that is grounded in data systematically gathered and analyzed" (Strauss & Corbin, 1998, p. 158). Using a constant comparative approach, the analysis first focused on a content analysis of each headteacher's experience to identify and code themes regarding challenges they experienced and strategies that they used. Using open coding (Gibbs, 2007; Huberman & Miles, 1994; Strauss & Corbin, 1998), the researchers categorized themes into a multilevel hierachy retaining access to subtheme details. They reviewed, compared, and coded transcripts several times, in a continual process of revising and refining the thematic categories (Lincoln & Guba, 1985) until they reached a point of saturation with sufficient organizational stability (Strauss, 1987). Building from the themes identified by a majority of the informants (a 50% case threshold), the researchers used axial coding to explore potential patterns between the challenge and strategy themes (Gibbs, 2007).

Trustworthiness

Several conditions and strategies ensured the trustworthiness of the research (Erlandson, Harris, Skipper, & Allen, 1993). The researchers' 10-year experience with Ugandan schools enhances credibility. Use of a 50% threshold for theme identification, participation of multiple coders, and peer debriefing among the researchers, one of whom has been a Ugandan headteacher, provided triangulation. Transferability of findings to educational contexts of other developing countries is sustained by a detailed description of sampling, descriptions of grounded themes and patterns, and inclusion of informant voices. Confirmabilility and freedom from bias are grounded by the 50% threshold for themes and patterns, the identifying conventions linking data to their sources, and the context-grounded explanations.

Limitations

The main limitation of this research is its use of localized data from a single district of the 80 in Uganda. While this limits generalization of the findings beyond this sample of headteachers, the richness of the thematic findings may allow headteachers in other Ugandan districts to transfer results (Erlandson et al., 1993). Transferability is more likely as all schools function under the same Ministry of Education, experience a similar mix of private and government schools, and operate under many of the same market pressures. Additionally, most secondary schools in the Mukono District provide boarding for students and draw directors, headteachers,

teachers, and students from across many districts and surrounding countries. The findings may also be transferable to new school leaders in other international contexts, particularly those with similarities in leader, teacher, and student mobility and in direct market-driven pressures on enrollment and performance. Another limitation of the study was the low proportion of female headteachers in the population and sample, which limited consideration of gender patterns on challenges and strategies. Additional limitations include conducting only a single interview with each participant and limiting informants to the headteachers themselves.

FINDINGS

The data revealed several themes and patterns in the challenges that faced a majority of the informants. The following section begins with a discussion of these themes, followed by a section dedicated to examining the strategies participants used to address challenges.

New Headteacher Challenges

Five themes emerged from the data that suggest liabilities of newness that may challenge school performance: navigating succession, managing school administration and limited resources, balancing diverse stakeholder needs, ensuring school academic performance, and surviving the competitive school environment. Over 75% of the informants identified these challenges and recognized accompanying threats to their success. Each of the following sections addresses a challenge.

Navigating succession. All participants felt unprepared, insufficiently informed, and challenged by the succession process. Such challenges were intensified because Uganda does not require that a headteacher hold a license, certificate, or degree; thus these new school leaders began their administrative careers with no formal training. Most private school headteachers were promoted from within the school. Margaret described how "the director was promoting me from class teacher to deputy, until he said, 'No, you should be the head of this institution.'" Charles also moved directly from teacher to headteacher:

> [In] the first school I headed … I hadn't been even a deputy head teacher. I was just picked from class and told to go head the school. So I knew nothing, how to run a staff meeting, how to budget, all those were challenges…. So I didn't know how, if I was faced with any question, I would answer that from parents, from children, or from teachers.

Lack of formal preparation was magnified in the private school context by lack of information about the school. Samuel said,

> [I] personally didn't receive mentorship from the person who occupied this office before me.... The former headteacher left giving me no information for me to carry on.... There was quite a gap. I just came in and started from scratch.

This gap contrasts with succession in government schools, in which a formal handover process marks the transition between school leaders. Thomas explained that "the former headteacher has to report the facilities and all the personnel, the students, debtors, and creditors, and the financial position to the incoming headteacher so [the new headteacher] will know where to start from."

New school leaders in both government and private schools experienced negative succession politics. Thomas' experience highlights the political challenge of achieving acceptance by a community that wanted someone else as headteacher:

> When I came for the handover ceremony, a lot of residents ... didn't want me to come. They had their own, a son of one of the senior citizens in the community, who was once a deputy headteacher here, and then he was promoted to the rank of acting headteacher [at another school]. They felt the time for their son is now. So people said "no" to any other person coming from elsewhere.

Internal political resistance was evident among school faculty and staff when the new school leader was an external appointment. Caroline recalled,

> When I first came, the members of staff resisted me. First they look at me as young. They have never known me before. To them, it was like strangers coming round. So initially picking up with them was a challenge.

Resistance increased when staff were loyal to the previous headteacher (e.g., Samuel noted that "the staff viewed my coming as a punishment to the one that went"). Disappointment was evident when a teacher or administrator at the school had expected the promotion. Edward recalled:

> The headteacher before had already gone, and the deputy was in charge of the school. So, my coming packed a threat for him. He was trying to sabotage work, like instigating students, like telling them they were supposed to be eating meat and rice, and they just got beans.... This deputy had to be moved away, but several times I would be ambushed on the way back home by people trying to harass me.

Reflecting the challenges of no preparation along with succession politics, findings support Charles's assertion that "a good culture of proper succession" is needed.

Managing school administration. All participants identified challenges of managing school administration (e.g., inherited administrative problems, limited resources, and administrative role ambiguity). Overcoming inherited problems was particularly challenging when headteachers were new to the school. Thomas found that "teachers had gone close to 7 months unpaid. The school was seriously indebted. Suppliers were not paid for what they had supplied, electricity bills and sorts." Some encountered debts caused by previous embezzlement of school funds, with suppliers demanding payment. Others inherited such challenges as poor school records, lack of budgets, untended physical facilities, uneven teacher quality, and poor student discipline.

All informants attributed limited resources, particularly financial resources, as due to nonpayment of school fees. They struggled between enrolling students with minimal government-guaranteed funding or students at higher fees that might not be paid. Physical resources were quite expensive and not easily available. Human resources were constrained by teacher turnover and the school's inability to pay teacher salaries. Peter struggled: "We are strained so much that sometimes the things that are important, we leave them out ... [we] want to do them, but we do not have the resources to achieve them." Headteachers spent much of their time managing finances, student enrollments, and payments of school fees.

Role ambiguity was another administrative challenge. Roles of headteacher and director were often unclear or at cross-purposes, with misaligned goals or unclear expectations. Jacob explained that "the breakdown we have had is in schools where the director wants to be the headteacher." The headteacher, closer to daily school functioning, was challenged when the director, having greater authority, made decisions without full information. Teachers or students often went to the director for something they wanted. John warned that "teachers will not respect this office if they know the director has power over you because once they discover this, they will start going to the director instead of you. Once that happens, you will lose control."

Role ambiguity also occurred between the headteacher and other school administrators. Roles needed to be clarified and respected to avoid overlap and confusion. The deputy headteacher over academics and the director of studies should take the active role in curriculum, teaching quality, and supervision, while the headteacher should manage other school issues. Jacob explained that one role of the headteacher is "defining the other subordinate officers' roles and making sure you don't overtake. You don't ambush other people's offices. So many times parents and students actually run to me for problems that should have been addressed by those [other] offices." An additional ambiguity of administrative roles is that the headteacher is also a teacher and, as such, is supervised by the director of studies.

Balancing diverse stakeholder needs. Participants struggled to meet the needs and expectations of three stakeholder groups: school directors, teachers, and parents. All stakeholders had interests in school survival and academic success, yet they had competing financial needs. School directors, who directly supervise the headteachers, own the schools and need profitability; teachers need salaries from the directors; and parents need to pay lower school fees (see Figure 3.2). School directors exercised great pressure on headteachers, whose jobs were at stake. These leaders felt the tension of sustaining the school while successfully balancing and advocating for the needs of these diverse stakeholders.

All new headteachers in the private schools knew that the directors, while valuing education, needed the school to be financially viable and hopefully profitable. Financial resources are obtained primarily through attracting fee-paying students who remain at the school and perform well on national exams. High performance on exams builds a school's reputation for quality, which serves to attract future fee-paying students. Thus a high-stakes challenge for new school leaders was negotiating the directors' financial needs while encouraging their continued financial investment in the school to ensure academic performance. Edward described this tension:

> Your dreams might not coincide with [the director] because … there are certain areas where there should be more investments, and the director might

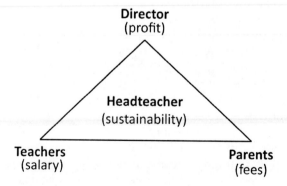

Figure 3.2.   Three key stakeholder groups with competing financial needs.

not agree. He has another dream of making money. And you find this brings a bit of friction because you are moving in different directions.

This friction directly affected teachers, as schools often did not pay teachers in a timely manner. Edward said, "[My] teachers are excellent. They want to work. But in most cases, we fall apart because of their remunerations." With delayed or unpaid teacher salaries, these new school leaders experienced teacher absenteeism, strikes, and high turnover. In Jacob's school, teachers withheld students' grades until they were paid. Headteachers were sympathetic to teachers' financial concerns. For example, James said, "I cry with them." However, these leaders were evaluated on student performance "regardless of whether [the] staff are suffering" (Matthew). Teachers frequently left the school in search of better-paying jobs or simply jobs that paid at all. Thus if the headteacher could not effectively advocate for teacher salaries, the long-term sustainability of school performance was threatened.

Parents as stakeholders sought to place their students in the best of the most affordable schools. With the importance of school fees, parents' school choice, and fee payment, these new school leaders needed to attract and retain parents who paid school fees. Fees, however, were dependent on sufficient academic progress. Peter reported, "If the kids don't study, they take home a different message to the parents. And if the parents see that nothing is happening in school, they will either move their kid or they will delay payment of school fees." School discipline also affected fee payment because "the board of governors fear that if you call their parents, these kids will be taken out, and the fees will be gone" (Paul). Headteachers constantly struggled with low-income parents who did not pay fees, realizing that if pressured they might transfer children from the school to avoid paying fees. Peter highlighted the role of parents in balancing stakeholder needs:

> Sometimes parents … are so [upset] why you have chased their kid back home for school fees. And then they are so [upset] why some teacher is not in class. And you want to help them understand that these things are related. If I don't chase you for fees, the teachers won't be in class. And if you do not pay, the kids won't learn. And [if] they are so hungry, you cannot do this…. We tell parents you have to look for the little money, however little it is. You have to pay because at the end of the day, we have costs to meet. And if your kid is going to class and they do not have textbooks, and the teachers are not paid, you will not be able to be happy because the school will not stand.

If parents did not pay fees, directors had insufficient resources to invest in the school and pay teachers. Thus these new headteachers were challenged to prioritize competing stakeholder needs, trying to benefit the school and students. But while the stakeholders had diverse financial needs, they held a common desire for academic performance.

Ensuring academic performance. Ensuring school performance on UNEB examinations was another challenge for new school leaders (90%). Thomas indicated, "The ultimate goal about the performance of the headteacher is the number of passing students at the end of the year." Without academic performance, schools had difficulty attracting fee-paying students Edward explained,

> People who have money cannot take their children to a school that has not made a name for itself, because [the scores] are published in the papers at the end of the year. Because if I have money, how can I expect to bring my child to a school that is not yet in the papers?

The quality of student admissions was a high strategic priority. To increase school quality, Susan suggested headteachers "be very careful as you are enrolling the students" to use their previous academic performance as a criterion. "If you get a student with a '4' [high mark] in Senior 1, you [can] expect that student to pass highly." Yet maintaining high student admission quality can interfere with the desire to increase enrollments to sustain school fees. Thus many headteachers faced the paradox of attracting a sufficient number of students without lowering the standards and threatening/compromising the school's academic performance.

Headteachers also had challenges in maintaining UNEB exam process quality. Difficulties such as cheating, verifying school residency, and acquiring quality exam materials (e.g., chemicals) could severely moderate a school's performance. For example, Steven was "called by the UNEB security council. They said our students received external assistance in the paper … and that was the reason why they had to withhold the results." The lack of exam results is very detrimental to a school's image.

To ensure academic performance, these new school leaders facilitated teaching quality, addressed student absenteeism, and managed student boarding. Teaching quality was challenged due to multiple nonacademic roles required of teachers in the school, teacher loyalty to the previous headteacher, unpredictability of teacher pay, teacher absenteeism, teacher strikes, and teacher turnover. Student absenteeism was frequent as students who could not pay school fees for a given term were "chased away" until they could return with fees. Students also avoided paying fees by "shifting" to another school each time payment was required. As a result, they could be absent for extended periods of time and have inconsistent preparation. School leaders also had to manage boarding for students who were preparing for the national exam and were often required to board at the school to increase study time and teacher access. Boarding created challenges such as providing sufficient food, maintaining appropriate relationships between male and female students, preventing illness due to close quarters, and preventing theft. Ensuring academic performance was critical in sustaining school viability in the highly competitive environment.

Surviving the competitive school environment. All informants identified the competitive environment as a major challenge. Intense competition resulted from the saturation of secondary schools and the high degree of parents' school choice, the low-income and resource-constrained context, and the dependence on school fees for critical school resources. In addition, some parents wanted their children to attend university, which required high performance on the national-level exit examinations. Thus secondary schools had to improve their image and reputation to compete for students, teachers, and educational resources.

Private schools suffered more resource disadvantage than did government-funded schools. It was crucial to attract students who would actually pay the school fees and attract competent teachers who would actually stay at the school. Headteachers struggled to keep school fees within a range that was competitive yet sufficient for school expenses. Susan explained, "As a private school, the more students you have, the more income; that is why students are our customers." New school leaders must convince directors to adopt lower fees to attract students while persuading parents to pay the school fees.

Small private schools had a particular challenge with obtaining payment of school fees. Normally, students who do not pay fees must be chased away from the school until they return with fees. However, Edward was frustrated that "when you try to chase them so you can get the money, they transfer. They go to other schools." James further explained this competitive challenge for his small private school, "When you take those big schools, they have the students. They have enough that even if you chase like 10, the school is not affected. Even if you discontinue 20, the school is not affected. But here, when you discontinue 20, you are going to run into an empty school."

Attracting/retaining teachers was also competitive. If pay was inadequate or inconsistent, teachers might seek part-time employment elsewhere or move to a more consistent school. James indicated that government schools have the advantage in retaining teachers because "they pay their teachers very well." Yet for a private school "a teacher can refuse to come to school. Why? Because you don't pay them promptly and you are paying them less [than government schools]." A school that could not attract and retain quality teachers would place its academic performance and thus its reputation at risk.

In summary, the five most prevalent challenges of these new headteachers had three commonalities. First, headteachers recognized that if these challenges were not met, the school's academic performance was threatened. Second, they actively sought strategies to address these challenges. But third, their liabilities of newness made these challenges difficult to address. They lacked personal experience, knowledge, and information about the role of headteacher; struggled with ineffective organizational systems; and suffered from underdeveloped relationships with critical stakeholders.

Strategies for Addressing the Challenges

The second research question focused on strategies new headteachers used to address these challenges. Four strategic themes emerged from the comments of a majority of informants: seeking advice and learning, actively communicating, building relationships, and enhancing school image.

Advice-seeking and learning. Woven through headteachers' strategies was the prevalent theme that they could not meet these challenges alone. They actively sought knowledge and advice from a variety of sources, including experienced mentors. Samuel said he "would definitely get in touch with [his] mentors.... I really think that what I have been able to achieve in this school has been mainly because of the mentorship I have received." Personal networks with other headteachers and sister schools provided information, feedback, advice, counsel, and emotional support. Steven described "ma[king] use of the other head teachers around us to help me out in case of an emergency," adding that they "helped to expose [me] to very many people, very many big offices." Headteachers also sought advice from members of their board of governors.

All informants belonged to the Mukono Headteacher Association (founded in 1999). John explained, "We have headteacher meetings where we share different issues. What[ever] I feel that is defeating me, I ask through my friend. 'How are you managing this? What do you do?' " Headteachers also visited other schools, teamed with other school administrators, went to the director for instruction, or referred to literature to tackle problems. They also turned to their own school faculty, staff, and administrators to gather information and seek advice.

Actively communicating. Active communication helped a majority of the informants to address their challenges. Steven explained that "it is from your communication that people are going to understand" and that they would arrive at "a solution for that thing that was appearing as a problem." Effective communication developed political understanding during succession and set clear expectations and vision for teachers. David described communicating with teachers after the handover meeting:

I told them that I've come here to work with you, and the school is not the headteacher's, but each of you own the school and you are responsible. I love people who are committed and devoted to work. So those who are devoted to work will be my best friends, and those who hate work will be my best enemy.

Communication was also important in persuading parents to pay school fees, attracting students, and creating positive school relations. Head-teachers negotiated school resources and advocated for the needs of teachers, as Edward explained,

The headteacher who brings the teachers' grievances and their cries to the director will always bridge the gap and minimize some of the tendencies of the director to over expect [financially] from schools because he will have the full picture.... He will go see the director and say, "If you go pick this much money from schools, it will create this problem." ... The headteacher who does this always makes the school grow and become successful. But the headteacher who does not do that will make the school collapse.

Communication was also necessary in effectively accomplishing the next two strategies of building relationships and enhancing the school's image.

Building relationships. The necessity for building relationships and networks was a strategic theme for 70% of the informants. Building relationships with stakeholders helped them to understand stakeholders' needs and to influence them. Study participants stressed the need to build good relationships with teachers and explained that effective relationships with parents would be necessary to sustain student enrollments and build the image of the school. They clearly recognized that their most critical relationships outside the school were with other headteachers, and they sought opportunities to strengthen these relationships.

Participants perceived building relationships as creating bridges for both learning and communication. David explained, "If teachers don't trust you, they take that back into their classes and it affects their attitude, which gets instilled into students, and then you can't have learning." New leaders who worked to reduce the gap between themselves and their teachers were able to build positive relationships of trust, which in turn created environments more conducive to learning (Hallam et al., 2009).

Enhancing school image. A majority of participants recognized the need to actively and consistently enhance the school's image. They engaged in public relations to protect and improve the image of the school, particularly in the local community. Thomas described what he had done:

I have tried to improve the image of the school by working closely with the local community. I regularly attend social functions in the community.... I also attend the funeral rites, wedding ceremonies, and the general functions around this place. I also try to cooperate with the primary and the feeder schools around.

Susan explained, "It is my responsibility to keep the image of the school. I have to protect it at whatever cost." John stressed that "in Uganda, we have very many schools, so it is competitive these days to run a secondary school. You need to have some very good marketing skills." Headteachers tried to use school strengths to attract students, and they encouraged teachers to be actively engaged in public relations for the school. John urged his teachers, "Let us all be marketing the school" and promised that "whenever you bring a student or persuade a student to come here, there is a commission." Headteachers also shared concerns that since their actions and those of teachers and staff could negatively affect the school's image, they had to be careful how they talked about the school, what information they shared with teachers and parents, and what strategies they used to chase students away for fees.

Using strategic patterns to address specific challenges. Although new school leaders in this study used several strategies, only three patterns emerged above the 50% case threshold, suggesting that they used certain strategies for specific challenges (see Table 3.3). First, communication was linked with managing school administration, specifically in regard to visioning with teachers and staff, negotiating administrative process and resource use, and building relationships.

Second, communication was used to help balance stakeholder needs, specifically in terms of negotiating with, advocating for, and persuading stakeholders. Third, the strategy of building school image directly addressed surviving in the competitive environment, specifically in terms of marketing, publicizing school performance on UNEB exams, and protecting school image through careful monitoring of actions and information sharing. As the informants explained their strategies, they recognized how these strategies had increased school performance or their ability to improve school performance.

DISCUSSION

The findings reflect the theoretical framework of strategic leadership portrayed in Figure 4.1 (Scott & Davis, 2007). Headteachers knew that their leadership could potentially influence school performance; however, this potential was moderated by their liabilities of newness (Baum, 1996;

Table 3.3. Number of Headteachers (*n* = 20) Using Particular Strategies to Address Specific Challenges

	Seek Advice and Learning	Actively Communicate	Build Relationships	Build School Image
Navigating succession	8	5	9	4
Managing school administration and limited resources	4	10*	6	5
Balancing stakeholder needs	3	13*	8	9
Ensuring school performance	2	6	2	7
Surviving the competitive environment	0	9	4	10*

*Above 50% case threshold.

Stinchcombe, 1965), including inexperience, inefficiency, or ineffectiveness, which created or exacerbated their main challenges or their abilities to address them (see Figure 3.3). First, new headteachers had to learn and practice new roles, such as negotiator, mediator, marketer, motivator, advocate, quality and resource controller, and politician. Their inexperience with these roles meant that addressing challenges required more time, effort, and political capital. These factors resulted in increased pressure and stress from having to learn on the job (Daresh & Playko, 1992). Second, many new headteachers had to develop new organizational systems, particularly school administrative systems to address teacher motivation, teacher quality, student discipline, marketing, resource acquisition, and resource management. Poor or nonexistent systems hindered their ability to effectively address the confronting challenges. Third, headteachers had to create and strengthen the social relationships necessary to access support, resources, information, and trust, as well as critical social and political capital. These relationships and resulting network structures require time to develop. Without these relationships, new headteachers were generally unable to receive the resources and help needed to effectively address challenges.

As illustrated in Figure 3.3, liabilities of newness experienced by new headteachers within the specific Ugandan educational context, particularly in terms of scarce resources and increasing market pressures, generated five strategic challenges that threatened school performance.

Headteachers faced political challenges in the succession process and administrative challenges of role ambiguity and limited resources. They were challenged in balancing diverse and often competing stakeholder needs and with ensuring high-level school performance in an extremely competitive educational environment. Future research needs to further explore specific relationships between liabilities of newness and these challenges.

Findings also suggest that while headteachers identified four main strategies for addressing their challenges, they did not always act strategically. Strategies were generally used across challenges, with only a few patterns suggesting that specific strategies targeted specific challenges. Headteachers' scaffolded strategies addressed challenges from three levels. At the first level, headteachers addressed their own personal development by seeking advice and learning, increasing their awareness and facilitation of other strategies. At the second level, they addressed interpersonal development through engaging in active communication and building relationships. These interpersonal strategies laid a necessary foundation for the third level, at which they focused on building school image. Findings suggest that using these strategies of personal development, interpersonal skills, and school image likely also served to address the underlying issues of their liabilities of newness as they learned new roles, developed new organizational systems, and built relationships. In all of their strategies, new headteachers did not act alone, but rather relied on, learned from, and collaborated with others. Future research

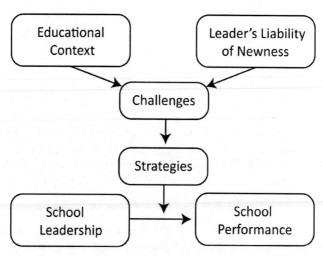

Figure 3.3.   The role of educational context and liabilities of newness on the effectiveness of new headteachers.

needs to examine how new headteacher strategies are acquired, developed, and sequenced; how particular strategies may be used for specific challenges and liabilities of newness; and how headteachers with different demographics (e.g., gender, tribal affiliation, etc.) experience and address their challenges.

IMPLICATIONS AND CONCLUSIONS

Headteachers in Uganda have the potential to influence school performance. Yet this potential may be diminished by challenges arising from specific educational contexts and from the liabilities of newness as they transition to their role as school leader. This research investigated how these new school leaders may perceive and seek to effectively address these challenges.

The Ugandan Ministry of Education may better support new headteachers by requiring, or at least providing, preparatory training. Skills of communication and relationship building should be addressed, as well as preparation for their strategic leadership role in improving school performance. Headteacher training should also inform new leaders of specific challenging contextual influences, including national education system requirements, stakeholder expectations, and other influences in the community environment. Training may help new headteachers to understand, reflect upon, and address their underlying liabilities of newness and to formulate and implement effective strategies to improve the performance of their schools.

Additionally, private schools may want to seek ways to enhance leadership "handoff" processes, learning from practices in government schools, and may want to find more formal transition support through the headteachers' association. In addition, school directors may want to reconsider the common practice of hiring new school leaders directly from the classroom. They might ease the transition by first moving teachers into other administrative roles such as director of study or deputy headteacher, helping to decrease their liabilities of newness when they are eventually promoted to headteacher.

This research also informs discussion about the intersection of economy and education. Much of the scholarly research and discourse in this area focuses on contexts such as the United States, where direct market pressures and competition for tuition-paying students are far less critical than in developing countries such as Uganda. This research can potentially initiate a more explicit discourse and investigation on the challenges and training needs of new headteachers in similarly challenged and competitive locations. While headteachers obviously valued high academic performance, they lived daily with the challenges of balancing academic with economic survival needs. Liabilities of newness may be further magnified in educational contexts of scarce resources, low financial support from government, and no preparation requirements for school leaders. School systems in other countries with contexts in which the interplay of education and economics creates intense pressures may find value in the challenges and strategies identified in this research. Future research needs to continue to examine differing educational contexts and their effects on the challenges and strategies of new school leaders.

Economically challenging and competitive educational contexts generate specific implications for a variety of stakeholders in the continual improvement of educational services. Governments may want to consider education policies that help school leaders effectively manage both the liabilities of newness they bring to leadership roles and the challenging paradox of economics and education. Ministries of education and district education leaders can tailor leadership preparation, both preliminary and ongoing, for the specific educational and cultural environment. Education researchers need to take into account how educational contexts differ, both in kind and in degree, realizing that context unavoidably matters-- and it matters deeply. Leadership strategies developed for a given context may not work for new school leaders across national or regional locations (Kitavi & van der Westhuizen, 1997; Memon & Bana, 2005). As researchers develop theory and explanations to support the development and success of new school leaders, they need to acknowledge important contextual differences, resisting the temptation to assume that apparent similarities are in fact equal conditions. Future research should continue to uncover and understand such vital contextual factors within and across national contexts.

As new school leaders acclimatize to a new role, their liabilities of newness are easily exposed. As a result, they must be strategic in both their actions and decisions if they are to lead effectively. This research suggests that new headteachers who seek advice, communicate, build relationships, and strengthen the school's image may be more effective at addressing the challenges of their liabilities of newness and their specific educational context. Ministries of education, universities, and other providers of leadership preparation, as well as new headteachers themselves, may benefit from this research to improve their educational systems. These better-informed and more contextually sensitive efforts will better enable both the academic performance and economic viability of schools, particularly in contexts such as Uganda.

REFERENCES

Ballinger, G. A., & Schoorman, F. D. (2007). Individual reactions to leadership succession in workgroups. *Academy of Management Review, 32*, 118–136.

Baum, J. A. C. (1996). Organizational ecology. In S. Clegg, C. Hardy, & W. Nord (Eds.), *Handbook of organization studies* (pp. 77–114). London: SAGE.

Cotton, K. (2003). *Principals and student achievement: What the research says.* Alexandria, VA: Association for Supervision and Curriculum Development.

Crow, G. M. (2006). Complexity and the beginning principal in the United States: Perspectives on socialization. *Journal of Educational Administration, 44*(4), 310–325.

Daresh, J. C., & Playko, M. A. (1992). *The professional development of school administrators: Pre-service, induction and in-service application.* Boston: Allyn & Bacon.

Daresh, J. C., & Playko, M. A. (1994). Aspiring and practicing principals: Perceptions of critical skills for beginning leaders. *Journal of Educational Administration 32*(2), 35–45.

Davies, B. J., & Davies, B. (2006). Developing a model for strategic leadership in schools. *Educational Management Administration & Leadership, 34*, 121–139.

Erlandson, D. A., Harris, E. L., Skipper, B. L., & Allen, S. D. (1993). *Doing naturalistic inquiry: A guide to methods.* Newbury Park, CA: SAGE.

Gibbs, G. R. (2007). *Analysing qualitative data.* Thousand Oaks, CA: SAGE.

Glaser, B., & Strauss, A. (1967). *The discovery of grounded theory: Strategies of qualitative research.* London: Wiedenfeld & Nicholson.

Hallam, P. R., Hite, J. M., Hite, S. J., & Mugimu, C. B. (2009). The development and role of trust in educational leadership: A comparative study of U. S. and Ugandan school administrators. In A. W. Wiseman & S. Silova (Eds.), *Educational leadership: Global contexts and international comparisons* (Vol. 11, pp. 49–81). Brighton, UK: Emerald Publishing.

Hallinger, P., & Heck, R. H. (1996). Reassessing the principal's role in school effectiveness: A review of empirical research, 1980–1995. *Educational Administration Quarterly, 32*(1), 5–44.

Hanna, D. P. (2001). *Leadership for the ages: Delivering today's results, building tomorrow's legacy.* Provo, UT: Executive Excellence Publishing.

Hite, J. M., & Hesterly, W. S. (2001). The evolution of firm networks: From emergence to early growth of the firm. *Strategic Management Journal, 22*(3), 275–286.

Hite, J. M., Hite, S. J., Jacob, W. J., Rew, W. J., Mugimu, C. B., & Nsubuga, Y. K. (2006). Building bridges for resource acquisition: Network relationships among headteachers In Ugandan private secondary schools. *International Journal of Education Development, 26*, 495–512.

Hite, J. M., Hite, S. J., Rew, W. J., Mugimu, C. B., & Jacob, W. J. (2009, March). Resource network centrality and school performance: Examining a secondary school network in Mukono, Uganda. Paper presented at the annual meeting of the Comparative International Education Society, Charleston, SC.

Hite, S. J., & De Grauwe, A. (2009). *Capacity development in educational planning and management for achieving EFA: Learning from successes and failures.* Paris: UNESCO/IIEP.

Hobson, A., Brown, E., Ashby, P., Keys, W., Sharp, C., & Bene?eld, P. (2003). *Issues for early headship: Problems and support strategies*. Nottingham, UK: National College for School Leadership.

Huberman, A. M., & Miles, M. B. (1994). Data management and analysis methods. In N. K. Denzin & Y. S. Lincoln (Eds.), *Handbook of qualitative research* (pp. 428–444). Thousand Oaks, CA: SAGE.

Kitavi, M. W., & Van Der Westhuizen, P. C. (1997). Problems facing beginning principals in developing countries: A study of beginning principals in Kenya. *International Journal of Educational Development, 17*(3), 251–263.

Leithwood, K., Seashore-Louis, K., Anderson, S., & Wahlstrom, K. (2004). *How leadership influences student learning*. New York: The Wallace Foundation.

LeTendre, B. G., & Roberts, B. (2005, November). *A national view of certification of school principals: Current and future trends*. Paper presented at the annual meeting of the University Council for Educational Administration, Nashville, TN.

Lincoln, Y., & Guba, E. (1985). *Naturalistic inquiry*. Beverly Hills, CA: Sage.

Lunenburg, F. C., & Irby, B. J. (2005). *The principalship: Vision to action*. Stamford, CT: Cengage Learning.

Marzano, R. J., Waters, J. T., & McNulty, B. A. (2005). *School leadership that works: From research to results*. Alexandria, VA: Association for Supervision and Curriculum Development.

Memon, M., & Bana, Z. (Eds.). (2005). *Pedagogical leadership in Pakistan: Two head-teachers from the northern areas*. Karachi, Pakistan: Oxford University Press.

Scott, W. R., & Davis, G. F. (2007). *Organizations and organizing: Rational, natural and open system perspectives*. Upper Saddle River, NJ: Prentice-Hall.

Stinchcombe, A. L. (1965). Organizations and social structure. In J. G. March (Ed.), *Handbook of organizations* (pp. 153–193). Chicago: Rand-McNally.

Strauss, A. L. (1987). *Qualitative analysis for social scientists*. New York: Cambridge University Press.

Strauss, A. L., & Corbin, J. (1998). *Basics of qualitative research: Techniques and procedures for developing grounded theory*. Thousand Oaks, CA: SAGE.

Tooms, A. (2007). An international effort to build leadership capacity: Insights from the first cohort of educational administration at The College of the Bahamas. *Journal of Research on Leadership Education, 2*, 1-41.

UNESCO. (2009). *Education for All Global Monitoring Report 2009: Overcoming inequality: Why governance matters*. Paris: Author.

CHAPTER 4

PROBLEMS REPORTED BY NOVICE HIGH SCHOOL PRINCIPALS

Sarah Beth Woodruff and Theodore J. Kowalski

INTRODUCTION

At the time the Elementary and Secondary Education Act (PL 107-110 and commonly known as the No Child Left Behind Act) was reauthorized in 2001, principals were being asked to restructure schools so that all students achieve adequate yearly progress (Bottoms, O'Neill, Fry, & Hill, 2003). Concurrently, however, policymakers in some states were eliminating or attenuating licensing requirements for this pivotal position (Anthes, 2004; Feistritzer, 2003). For at least the last few decades, educational administration scholars, such as Hallinger and Heck (1996) and Murphy (2003), warned that permitting underqualified persons to be principals was myopic policy.

Though multiple factors underlie efforts to deprofessionalize school administration, the absence of social authority is arguably the one that has made the education profession most vulnerable (Elmore, 2007). Critics, such as Hess (2003), claim that traditional state licensing require-

The Challenges for New Principals in the Twenty-First Century:
Developing Leadership Capabilities Through Professional Support, pp. 77–100
Copyright © 2010 by Information Age Publishing
All rights of reproduction in any form reserved.

ments, such as teaching experience and graduate degrees in educational administration, have had little or no effect on school improvement. Moreover, they believe that employing noneducators with management training would make schools more efficient and possibly more effective. The only evidence they have provided to support this contention, however, has been anecdotal accounts of business executives, politicians, or retired military officers serving as superintendents in large urban districts (Kowalski, 2004).

The study of novice high school principals reported in this chapter was based on the premise that the education profession needs to establish social authority in order to survive. Arguably, the initial step in meeting this need is to validate an essential knowledge base substantiating the social benefit of practitioner licensing. Specifically, the research focused on the following objectives:
{BL}

- Developing a profile of Ohio novice high school principals
- Developing a profile of the schools in which they were employed
- Determining perceptions of the frequency and severity of problems identified by the study population
- Determining levels of possible association between the frequency of problems identified and selected individual and school demographic variables.

First, a theoretical context for the issues addressed in the study is provided, especially in relation to characteristics of novice principals and the problems they encounter. Then the Ohio study is described and findings are reported. Finally, conclusions are shared and recommendations made for additional research. Overall, outcomes reported here do not support assertions that teaching experience and academic preparation in educational administration are unessential requirements for licensing—and hence for entering practice.

THEORETICAL FRAMEWORK

Principals and Professionalism

Since the late 1980s, numerous authors (e.g., Daresh, 2006; Datnow & Castellano, 2001; Goldring & Rallis, 1993; Heck & Hallinger, 1999; Murphy, 2002) have emphasized the crucial role principals must play in improving low-performing schools. In fact, state accountability systems place the "burden of school success and individual achievement squarely on the principal's shoulders" (Bottoms et al., 2003, p. 5). Yet, several policy papers published earlier this decade (e.g., Broad Foundation & Thomas B. Fordham Institute, 2003; Hess, 2003) promoted deregulating practice in school administration—a decision that would eliminate or make voluntary long-standing licensing requirements (Kowalski, 2004).

In professions, preservice academic preparation has focused on developing knowledge and skills thought to be essential for entering practice. Logically, this knowledge base should be validated by practice-based research examining experiences in the first year of autonomous practice. Practice-based research is predicated on the conviction that only some aspects of problems and contextual variables are unique. This perspective elevates the need to integrate theory and practice, primarily by conducting research that tests and refines theory in the context of practice-based problems. Thus, practice-based research is defined as inquiry that integrates theoretical, technical, and practical knowledge domains (Oancea & Furlong, 2007). In school administration, however, relatively little research has been practice-based (Elmore, 2007; Levin, 2006) or focused on first-year practitioners (Kowalski, Place, Edmister, & Zigler, 2009). Heck and Hallinger (2005) posit that philosophical differences toward research among school administration professors have resulted in an ever-widening range of studies, many of which have little or nothing to do with practice. Concurrently, many policymakers believe that most school administrators have failed to apply empirical evidence to their practice, thus negating the potential benefits of their academic preparation (Kowalski, 2009).

Novice High School Principals

More is known about high school principals generally than about novice high school principals specifically. Data reported by the National Center for Education Statistics (NCES, 2007) for 2003–04 revealed that there were only slightly more male principals (50.3%) than female principals (49.7%) across all types (public and private) and levels (elementary and secondary) of schools. However, between 1993–94 and 2003–04, the percentage of female principals in public schools increased from 14 to 26% in secondary schools. Kerrins (2001), Ortiz (1982), and others (Ozga, 1993; Ruhl-Smith, Shen, & Cooley, 1999) found that generally women move into administration at a later point in their careers and have more classroom experience than their male peers. Furthermore, other researchers (Adams & Hambright, 2004; Loder & Spillane, 2005; Shakeshaft, 1999) found that women, more frequently than men, transition to the position of assistant principal or central office administrator rather than directly to a head building principalship at the secondary school level.

Overwhelmingly, most principals in 2003–04 were white non-Hispanics (82%); only 9% did not have a graduate degree and 34% had advanced graduate degrees (above a master's degree), with 8% having doctoral degrees (NCES, 2007). According to relatively recent research conducted by Rodriguez-Campos, Rincones-Gomez, and Shen (2005), the typical high school principal was male; in 2000, the National Association of Secondary School Principals (NASSP, 2001) found females comprised 20% of high school principals.

Much of what has been written about novice principals generally and about novice high school principals specifically has been based on opinion (e.g., promoting mentoring, designing induction-year programs). Even demographic data regarding the latter population are difficult to locate. In one of the few articles addressing first-year high school principals, Rodriguez-Campos and associates (2005) found that only 10% of them had entered the position with fewer than 3 years of teaching experience and many had relatively little previous administrative experience. They found this to be particularly prevalent among novice principals in rural schools, where 62% had no prior administrative experience; the latter finding is similar to data reported by Kerrins (2001).

Historically, novice high school principals have been employed in high-challenge positions. Most notably, a majority has been employed in schools that (1) were small in terms of enrollment (e.g., Alvy, 1983; NCES, 1997), (2) had a high percentage of economically disadvantaged students (e.g., Gates, Ringel, & Santibanez, 2003; Ohio Department of Education, 2005; Rodriguez-Campos et al., 2005), (3) had no assistant principals (Rodriguez-Campos et al., 2005), and (4) were in low socioeconomic status districts—that is, districts with below-average assessed valuations per pupil (Ohio Department of Education, 2005).

Entry to Practice

Logically, the relevancy and adequacy of professional preparation affect the nature and frequency of problems encountered by novice principals (Hale & Moorman, 2003; Leithwood & Riehl, 2003). Yet, licensing standards (Anthes, 2004; Feistritzer, 2003; Kowalski, in press) and academic preparation (Alvy & Robbins, 2005; Hale & Moorman, 2003; Jackson & Kelley, 2002; Kowalski, 2010) for these administrators vary substantially among and within states. Continuing dissimilarities among professional preparation programs demonstrate that neither accreditation nor national standards[1] have produced uniformity—a fact that supports the contention that policy governing the preparation and licensing of administrators remains more political than professional (Kowalski, 2008). By regulating school administration politically rather than professionally (as is done in other professions), policymakers arguably jeopardize the welfare of communities (Cochran-Smith, 2005) and discourage the education profession from continuously seeking self-improvement (Herrington & Wills, 2005).

Research on principal preparation typically has reported problems related to curricular relevance (e.g., Bottoms & O'Neill, 2001; Davis, Darling-Hammond, LaPointe, & Meyerson, 2005; Milstein & Krueger, 1997; NASSP, 2001; Waters & Grubb, 2004; Young, Peterson, & Short, 2002), an expected outcome given pervasive dissimilarities in the quantity and quality of preparation provided. Equally predictable, many studies (e.g., Farkas, Johnson, & Duffett, 2004; Farkas, Johnson, Duffett, & Foleno, 2001; Herr, 2002; Institute for Educational Leadership, 2000; Peterson, 2002; Thompson & Legler, 2003) have recommended improvements for preservice preparation.

Interestingly, studies including only novice principals or those that separated responses for novices and experienced principals (e.g., Daniel, Kyle, & Ulrich, 2005; National Association of Elementary School Principals, 1979) have generally reported that first-time principals rated their academic preparation as effective.[2] Despite variations in satisfaction with preservice preparation, many authors (Bottoms & O'Neill, 2001; Davis et al., 2005; Milstein & Krueger, 1997; NASSP, 2001; Waters & Grubb 2004; Young et al., 2002) have concluded that preparation deficiencies should not be addressed by deregulating current requirements.

Doubts about the need to license school administrators were rekindled in relation to public dissatisfaction with schools. Reservations about continuing to require a state license to practice--and hence, to require academic preparation—centers largely on four issues.

1. The perception that there is or will be a critical shortage of qualified principals
2. The ability of traditionally prepared principals to respond adequately to demands for increased school accountability and efficiency
3. The extent to which states should regulate public administration, including administration in schools and districts
4. The contention that current requirements prevent or discourage competent managers outside of education from becoming superintendents and principals (Kowalski, 2004, 2009).

Currently, four states no longer require principals to be licensed, and 18 others have provisions for obtaining alternative certification or licensing (Anthes, 2004).

Problems of Practice

School characteristics such as size (student enrollment), geographic location (e.g., rural, urban) and type (elementary or secondary) are thought to be associated with types of problems encountered by principals. As examples, VanderJagt, Shen, and Hsieh (2001) found that secondary school administrators reported more severe and more prevalent problems than did elementary school principals; urban school principals reported more severe and frequent problems than did rural school principals; and principals of larger schools reported more frequent and severe problems than did those in smaller schools.

A comprehensive search of extant literature on novice principals yielded a substantial number of journal articles, conference papers, books, government and commission reports, doctoral dissertations, and other documents published since 1960. Nevertheless, most of these publications address socialization and professional preparation rather than problems of practice. Moreover, most of the research reported was qualitative, having been conducted with few subjects and based on interviewing or storytelling techniques (e.g., Tredway, Brill, & Hernandez, 2007). Though the amount of research conducted on the principalship overall has been extensive, the amount conducted on problems of practice has been surprisingly limited (Walker & Carr-Stewart, 2006). Moreover, research on problems experienced by novices has been especially inadequate. Arguably, the three most notable researchers contributing to the knowledge base in this area have been Daresh (Daresh, 1986; Daresh & Male, 2000; Daresh & Playko, 1989, 1992, 1993), Parkay (Parkay, Currie, & Rhodes, 1992; Parkay & Hall, 1992), and Alvy (Alvy, 1983; Alvy & Coladarci, 1985; Alvy & Robbins, 2005). Collectively, their findings indicate that novice principals commonly experience anxiety, frustration, alienation, and self-doubt.

Unfortunately, research does not provide a clear indication as to whether problems encountered by novices are dissimilar to those encountered by their experienced peers. Several researchers (e.g., Cave & Wilkinson, 1992; Greenfield, 1995; Walker & Carr-Stewart, 2006) found notable differences between the two groups, whereas others (e.g., Billot, 2003; Brimm, 1983; Dunning, 1996; Howell, 1981; Lyons, 1999; Muse & Thomas, 1991; Portin & Shen, 1998) did not. Studies that have not separated findings for the two groups (Billot, 2003; Dunning, 1996; Howell,

1981; Lyons, 1999; Muse & Thomas, 1991; Portin & Shen, 1998) report the most frequently identified problems as (1) workload; (2) compliance with state and federal policies and mandates; (3) time commitment and time management; (4) staffing issues, including teacher quality concerns and evaluation; (5) paperwork and meetings; and (6) decision making. Studies that have included only novice and second-year principals (Alvy & Coladarci, 1985; Daresh, 1986; Walker, Mitchell, & Turner, 1999) report problems in areas such as (1) role clarification, (2) limitations on technical expertise, (3) supervision of instruction, (4) personnel management, and (5) socialization (both to the profession and to the workplace). In light of inconsistent results regarding problems of practice, Kruger, van Eck, and Vermeulen (2005) and Walker and Carr-Stewart (2006) caution that perceptions of self-efficacy and school climate may influence if and how novice and experienced principals admit to encountering problems.

THE OHIO STUDY

Methodology

The study population included 25 novice high school principals who completed their first year in the position during the 2006–07 school year. In 2006, there were 636 (noncharter) public high schools in Ohio, and between the end of the 2005–06 school year and the beginning of the 2006–07 school year, 29% changed principals. The list of new principals was analyzed, and data verified that 25 on this list were persons who had not been employed previously as principals (though some had been assistant principals).

The study was descriptive and relied on survey research to collect quantitative data regarding principals' perceptions. The instrument, specifically designed for this study, contained 48 items related to problems of practice. The *Ohio Standards for Principals* (Ohio Department of Education, 2006) were adapted to develop items related to problems of practice, and items related to personal problems were compiled from an extensive review of relevant research on the principalship. A reliability estimate (Cronbach alpha) was calculated for the instrument using scale items to test for internal consistency; the reliability of the instrument when used with the study population was 0.95.

State education database records provided demographic data for the study population and the schools in which they were employed. Though the response rate for the surveys was 21 of 25 or 84%, the demographic profile is based on the entire study population. Personal demographic data collected from the surveys were merely used to validate state records.

All data, both state records and surveys, were collected and analyzed between October 2007 and February 2008.

Data regarding the frequency and severity of problems of practice were analyzed in a variety of ways. Primary data analysis consisted of a descriptive analysis and ranking of resulting means and sum totals to ascertain what respondents perceived to be their most frequent and most severe problems of practice. Additionally, the frequency means for five composite variables, one representing each of the *Ohio Standards for Principals*, were calculated and compared to determine which standards were most and least frequently problematic.

Data were analyzed further to explore the possible relationship between respondents' perceptions of problems and selected individual and school characteristics. Groups were created for each demographic variable (e.g., gender groups were male and female) and all respondents were categorized. After assigning all respondents to a group, group mean values were calculated. Correlation coefficients were calculated and used descriptively as prescribed by Chen and Popovich (2002) and Cohen and Cohen (1983) to determine the strength of association between each group's mean problem frequency score and group membership.

FINDINGS

Study Population Profile. The typical member of the study population was a 43-year-old male with slightly more than 10 years of teaching experience and 4 years of assistant principal experience. He had completed a professional principal preparation program and held an Ohio professional (5-year) principal license. He had completed 15 or more semester hours of graduate school credits beyond a master's degree and became a principal (not including assistant principal) approximately 5 years after being licensed. Only 5 of the 25 Ohio novices were women and only 5 of the 25 were under age 35. Specific data for the personal profile is presented in Table 4.1.

Profile of Employing Schools. The typical employing school included Grades 9–12, enrolled fewer than 750 students, and had a higher percentage of economically disadvantaged students than the average Ohio high school. The school was professionally staffed by 50 teachers and an assistant principal, and was located in rural (40%) or urban (40%) areas. Employing schools with fewer than 500 students typically had no assistant principal. Specific data for the employing school profile is presented in Table 4.2.

Frequency and Severity of Problems. Means for problem frequency ranged from 0 (*never a problem*) to 3 (*always a problem*). Of the 10 problems of

Table 4.1.   Ohio Novice
High School Principal Demographic Characteristics

Demographic Characteristic	n	Frequency	Percent
Gender			
Female	25	5	20
Male	25	20	80
Age			
Under 35 years of age	25	5	20
Not under 35 years of age	25	20	80
Years of teaching experience			
0–5 years	21	4	19.0
6–10 years	21	8	38.1
11–15 years	21	6	28.6
16–20 years	21	3	14.3
Years of assistant principal experience			
0 years	21	5	23.8
1–3 years	21	4	19.0
4–7 years	21	10	47.6
8–12 years	21	1	4.8
More than 12 years	21	1	4.8
Principal license type			
Provisional license	25	5	20
Professional license	25	18	72
Alternative license	25	2	8
Highest level of academic attainment			
Master's degree	21	1	4.8
Master's degree + 15 semester hours	21	8	38.1
Master's degree + 30 semester hours or EdS	21	12	57.1

**Table 4.2.   Ohio Novice
High School Principal School
Demographic Characteristics (N = 25)**

Demographic characteristic	Frequency	Percent
Grade levels		
Grades 7–12	7	28.0
Grades 9–12	17	68.0
Grades 10–12	1	4.0
Student enrollment		
Fewer than 350 students	7	28.0
350–749 students	8	32.0
750–999 students	6	24.0
1,000–1,499 students	3	12.0
More than 1,499 students	1	4.0
School type		
Rural/agricultural-High poverty	4	16.0
Rural/agricultural-Low poverty	3	12.0
Rural/small town-Moderate median income	3	12.0
Urban-High poverty	10	40.0
Urban/suburban-Low poverty	5	20.0

practice that novices reported encountering more frequently (see Table 4.3), six were personal-type problems: (1) time commitment, (2) workload management, (3) effects on personal life, (4) effects on family life, (5) maintaining a healthy lifestyle, and (6) inadequate compensation. The remaining four were professional-type problems, so characterized by the *Ohio Standards for Principals*: (1) monitoring implementation of academic content standards, (2) identifying and allocating resources, (3) engaging stakeholders in the change process, and (4) visiting classrooms and providing feedback on instruction. Of 40 potential problems of practice included on the survey, all but two were found to be problematic at least sometimes; however, no problem was found to be problematic at all times.

A core set of items was described by all respondents to be problematic, but at varying frequencies (see Table 4.4). Two items regarding working with teachers (supervising and evaluating staff and using Standards for Teaching Profession to support teachers' growth) were rated by all respondents as either problematic *some of the time* or *often*. Similarly, 16 items were not reported to be *always* problematic by any respondent.

Table 4.3.   Frequency of Problems Reported by Ohio Novice High School Principals (*n* = 21)

Potential Problems of Practice	M	SD	Variance
Committing time to all job responsibilities	1.81	.750	.562
Managing the workload	1.67	.658	.433
Effects on personal life	1.62	.590	.348
Effects on family life	1.62	.590	.348
Maintaining a healthy lifestyle	1.62	.669	.448
Monitoring implementation of academic content standards	1.43	.598	.357
Identifying and allocating resources	1.43	.811	.657
Feeling adequately compensated for the job	1.43	.870	.757
Engaging stakeholders in the change process	1.38	.590	.348
Visiting classrooms and providing feedback on instruction	1.38	.669	.448

Table 4.4.   Items Identified as Problematic by All Ohio Novice High School Principals (*n* = 21)

Potential Problems of Practice
Effects on personal life
Engaging stakeholders in the change process
Supervising and evaluating staff
Committing time to all job responsibilities
Visiting classrooms and providing feedback on instruction
Using *Standards for Teaching Profession* to support teachers' growth
Effects on family life
Managing the workload

Five subscales, one for each of the *Ohio Standards for Principals*, were created and analyzed independently. Composite mean values for the problem frequency of each standard were rank-ordered and reported for all five standards (see Table 4.5). The value for each composite mean ranged from 0 (*never a problem*) to 3 (*always a problem*). Problems described by the *Ohio Standards for Principals*, Standard 2, Instruction, were identified as being the most frequently problematic for the novices. Principals also reported frequent problems with Ohio Standard 1, Continuous Improvement, which describes tasks related to planning and visioning. Novices reported few problems with Ohio Standard 4, Collaboration, which includes communicating and maintaining interpersonal relations.

**Table 4.5.   Frequency of Problems Associated With
Ohio Standards for Principals (*n* = 21)**

Composite Variables	# No. of Items	M	SD	Variance
Ohio principal standard 2 Instruction	7	1.26	.409	.167
Ohio principal standard 1 Continuous improvement	6	1.19	.475	.226
Ohio principal standard 3 School operations, resources, and learning environment	10	1.14	.481	.232
Ohio principal standard 5 Parents and community engagement	5	1.13	.245	.297
Ohio principal standard 4 Collaboration	4	1.01	.527	.278
All problems of practice	40	1.23	.388	.150

The Ohio Standards, however, do not include personal dimensions of practice, many of which were frequently problematic.

Typically, problems identified as being frequent also were identified as being severe (see Table 4.6). Five points were awarded for a ranking of 1 (*most severe*), 4 points for a ranking of 2 (*second most severe*), and so on. Items not ranked by a respondent were awarded a zero. The most notable severe problems were related both to personal stressors (e.g., time, workload, effects on personal and family life, and inadequate compensation) and professional responsibilities (e.g., supervision and evaluation of staff, resource allocation, and compliance and monitoring related to state and federal mandates). Several items were not identified by any respondent as among their most severe problems of practice. These data indicated that novice principals did not experience severe problems with administrative responsibilities, such as budgeting and using data for a variety of purposes, or with interpersonal relations and communication with a range of stakeholders.

Problems of Practice and Selected Demographic Variables. Groups were created for each demographic variable and each respondent was categorized accordingly. Group average problem frequency scores were calculated from individual respondent mean problem scores. Group sizes and average problem frequency scores are reported in Table 4.7 for selected demographic variables.

Group average problem frequency scores were correlated with group membership categories utilizing point-biserial (r_{pb}) and eta (η) correlation

**Table 4.6.   Problems Deemed Most Severe by
Ohio Novice High School Principals (*n* = 21)**

Potential Problems of Practice	Rank	Sum*	M	SD
Committing time to all job responsibilities	1	46	2.19	2.04
Managing the workload	2	24	1.14	1.32
Feeling adequately compensated for the job	3	21	1.00	1.58
Effects on family life	4 (tie)	20	0.95	1.50
Effects on personal life	4 (tie)	20	0.95	1.66
Maintaining a healthy lifestyle	5 (tie)	18	0.86	1.59
Helping teachers understand academic content standards	5 (tie)	18	0.86	1.71
Consistently applying behavioral policies, procedures, and rules	6	16	0.76	1.67
Engaging stakeholders in the change process	7	15	0.71	1.68
Complying with local, state, and federal mandates	8 (tie)	14	0.67	1.46
Identifying and allocating resources	8 (tie)	14	0.67	1.49
Monitoring implementation of academic content standards	9	12	0.57	1.47
Supervising and evaluating staff	10	11	0.52	1.21

* Maximum possible value for sum was 105.

**Table 4.7.   Ohio Novice High School Principal
Group Mean Problem Scores (*n* = 21)**

Demographic Categories	Frequency	Average Problem Frequency Score
Gender		
Female	5	1.21
Male	16	1.24
Years of teaching experience		
0–5 years	4	0.97
6–10 years	8	1.11
11–15 years	6	1.30
16–20 years	3	1.76

Table continues on next page.

Table 5.7.   Continued

Demographic Categories	Frequency	Average Problem Frequency Score
Years of assistant principal experience		
0 years	5	1.54
1–3 years	4	1.32
4–7 years	10	0.98
8–12 years	1	1.35
More than 12 years	1	1.73
Student enrollment		
Fewer than 350 students	5	1.34
350–749 students	6	1.33
750–999 students	6	1.03
1,000–1,499 students	3	1.18
More than 1,499 students	1	0.83
School type*		
Rural/agricultural-High poverty	2	1.24
Rural/agricultural -Low poverty	3	1.33
Rural/small town-Moderate median income	3	1.37
Urban-High poverty	8	1.25
Urban/suburban-Low poverty	5	1.06

* School type is based on Ohio School Accountability typology definitions.

coefficients. Correlation coefficient values are reported without a positive or negative sign since special cases of the Pearson correlation coefficient (r) cannot be used to describe the direction of association (Chen & Popovich, 2002).

The following rubric prescribed by Cohen and Cohen (1983) was used to determine strength of association:

- Small association: correlations from .01 to .29
- Moderate association: correlations from .30 to .49
- Large association: correlations of .50 and higher

The associations between average problem frequency scores and all selected individual and school demographic variables are reported in Table 4.8. Large and nearly equivalent associations were found between the frequency of problems reported and two personal demographic variables,

Table 4.8.   Association of Problem Frequency With Ohio Novice High School Principal and School Demographics

Demographic Characteristic	Association With Problem Frequency		Strength of Association
	Correlation Coefficient		
	η	r_{pb}	
Gender	–	.04	Small
Teaching experience	.65	–	Large
Assistant principal experience	.68	–	Large
School size	.40	–	Moderate
School type	.28	–	Small

teaching experience and assistant principal experience. A moderate association was found between frequency of problems and school size (student enrollment). Small associations were found between problem frequency and gender, and problem frequency and school type.

CONCLUSIONS

Based on findings and existing knowledge, five primary conclusions were drawn:

1. Though demographic data about novice high school principals are limited, findings reported here suggest that the Ohio study population was representative of novice high school principals nationally. Specifically, the members appeared typical with respect to (1) age (e.g., Alvy & Coladarci, 1985), (2) gender (e.g., NASSP, 2001), and (3) quantity of professional preparation (e.g., Kerrins, 2001; Rodriguez-Campos et al., 2005). Females in this study population, however, had slightly less teaching experience and assistant principal experience than did their male peers—an atypical condition when considered in relation to other studies (e.g., Kerrins, 2001; Ortiz, 1982; Ozga, 1993; Shakeshaft, 1999). The profile of the employing schools appeared typical with respect to (1) school enrollment (e.g., Alvy, 1983; NCES, 1997) and (2) percentages of economically disadvantaged students enrolled (e.g., Gates et al., 2003; Rodriguez-Campos et al., 2005).

2. Findings on the employing schools support contentions that novices often are employed in highly challenging positions (see, e.g.,

Gates et al., 2003; Ohio Department of Education, 2005; Rodri-guez-Campos et al., 2005). That is, they are likely to be in small schools with restricted resources (both material and human) serv-ing relatively high percentages of economically disadvantaged stu-dents. This persisting trend may indicate that many first-time principals are willing to take less desirable positions to enter this level of administration.

3. The nature and frequency of problems identified by the Ohio nov-ices were typical of those reported in previous studies. For exam-ple, findings here reaffirmed previous research (Billot, 2003; Dunning, 1996; Howell, 1981; NASSP, 2001; Shen, Cooley, & Wegenke, 2004; Walker et al., 1999; Yerkes & Guaglianone, 1998) indicating that the most frequent problems related to administra-tive responsibilities or constraints. Three of the most frequently identified problems in this study also were identified as such in previous studies. They are (1) instructional supervision (e.g., Quong, 2006), (2) adjustment to the position (e.g., Kruger et al., 2005), and (3) managerial responsibilities (e.g., Portin & Shen, 1998). Findings reported here, however, indicated that overall the number of problems reported were fewer than those reported in some other studies (e.g., Daresh & Male, 2000; Farkas et al., 2004; Lyons, 1999). Moreover, personal-type problems were more fre-quently reported here than in some previous studies (e.g., Brimm, 1983; NASSP, 2001; Parkay et al., 1992).

4. The fourth conclusion is based on a discernible association between prior professional experience and the reported frequency of problems. Novices who had more years of teaching experience identified problems with greater frequency than did novices with fewer years of teaching experience. Likewise, novices who had more experience as an assistant principal identified problems with greater frequency than did novices who lacked this experience. Logically, one might assume that experience reduces problem fre-quency. Yet findings reported here and in other studies (e.g., Alvy & Coladarci, 1985; Hallinger & McCary, 1990; Leithwood & Stager, 1986) suggest otherwise. Specifically, it appears that experi-ence may enhance one's ability (by virtue of tacit knowledge) and willingness (by virtue of confidence) to admit that problems occur. In this vein, Alvy and Coladarci (1985) posited that prior experi-ence as an assistant principal heightened awareness of practice-based problems.

5. Outcomes reported here raise legitimate concerns about deregulat-ing practice in the principalship. As a prime example, deregulation

would allow persons with little or no teaching experience to occupy the position—a condition that may diminish the ability of these persons to identify and solve problems of practice. Knowledge of the content and context of a problem, obtained through experience, enhances an individual's ability to engage in focused problem-finding (Peterson, Murphy, & Hallinger, 1987). As Hallinger and McCary (1990) noted, strategic thinking and problem-solving processes are necessary instructional leadership skills acquired through academic study and experience. Studying aspiring principals, Copland (2000) found that exposure to problem-based learning (during principal internship courses) enhanced one's capability to frame problems of practice accurately.

DISCUSSION

Professions are essentially "occupations with special power and prestige. Society grants these rewards because professions have special competence and esoteric bodies of knowledge linked to central needs and values of the social system" (Larson, 1977, p. x). They customarily enjoy a symbiotic relationship with societies; that is, in return for services rendered, their practitioners are granted influence and social status. The scope of professional knowledge required for practice and the manner in which knowledge and skills are acquired have become increasingly important in a society where practitioners are expected to be near perfect (May, 2001). As an example, malpractice suits in medicine often reflect the expectation that a practitioner should have integrated empirical evidence, clinical expertise, and patient values in making consequential decisions (Kowalski, 2009).

In deciding what should be done to enhance principal effectiveness, state policymakers have been more inclined to attenuate existing licensing standards than to raise them. This trend contradicts literature identifying a principal's instructional leadership as a pivotal factor in school improvement (e.g., Duke, 1987; Greenfield, 1995; Hallinger & Heck, 1996; Leithwood & Jantzi, 2000; Leithwood & Riehl, 2003; Reynolds, 2002; Rutherford, Hord, & Thurber, 1984). In their meta-analysis of school improvement, Waters, Marzano, and McNulty (2003) found a significant relationship between school leadership and student achievement and concluded that effective leaders not only know what to do, but how, when, and why to do it. Leithwood and Stager (1986) also found that some variation in school effectiveness may be accounted for by the principal's ability to select and direct attention to the right problems. Marks and Printy (2003) found that while shared instructional leadership positively influenced school performance, principal leadership was necessary to achieve high-quality teaching and learning. And though Elmore (2003) concurs that leadership can be distributed in schools, he states that improvements in school performance hinge on the leader's ability to recognize problems and direct focus on targets for improvement. In summary, scholars familiar with the realities of schooling (Elmore, 2003; Hallinger & Heck, 1996; Leithwood & Jantzi, 2007; Leithwood & Riehl, 2003; McGuire, 2002; Waters et al., 2003) share two critical conclusions: (1) unless principals have the ability to frame classroom problems accurately, they are unlikely to help teachers improve instruction and (2) the ability to frame classroom problems accurately requires both theoretical knowledge (acquired via academic study) and tacit knowledge (acquired through practitioner experience).

Rather than disputing the publications of these respected scholars, deregulation advocates, such as the authors of *Better Leaders for America's Schools: A Manifesto* (Broad Foundation & Thomas B. Fordham Institute, 2003), simply have argued that the principal need not be an instructional expert. In support of this position, they posit that relatively little of what principals do relates directly to instruction. In stating his case for deregulation, Hess (2003) concedes that some schools may require principals who can function as instructional leaders, simply because they do not have access to essential support staff. As demonstrated in this and other studies, however, novices usually begin practice in limited-resource, high-problem schools.

In looking forward, policymakers should refrain from making emotional or political decisions that will make it even more difficult to restructure low-performing schools. If principal preparation and licensing are inadequate, and some education scholars believe that they are, reforming preparation rather than abandoning it is a more prudent choice. As demonstrated in this study, many problems encountered by first-time principals related to instructional leadership. Moreover, experience in schools appears to have made novice principals more conscious of problems that affect school improvement. In light of such outcomes, assuming that persons who have never studied pedagogy or taught students would be effective novice principals is illogical.

In conclusion, members of the profession have an obligation to involve themselves in critical policy decisions. Their influence, though, will depend on their empirical rather than political contributions. By conducting more practice-based research on novice principals and by sharing their findings with policymakers, they are more likely to expose the perils of deregulation (Kowalski et al., 2009).

REFERENCES

Adams, K. L., & Hambright, W. G. (2004). Encouraged or discouraged?: Women teacher leaders becoming principals. *The Clearing House, 77*, 209–211.

Alvy, H. (1983). The problems of new principals. *Dissertation Abstracts International, 44*(03), 1979A. (UMI No. 8326696)

Alvy, H., & Coladarci, T. (1985). Problems of the novice principal. *Research in Rural Education, 3*(1), 39–47.

Alvy, H., & Robbins, P. (2005). Growing into leadership. *Educational Leadership, 62*(8), 50–54.

Anthes, K. (2004, April). *Administrator license requirements, portability, waivers, and alternative certification.* ECS State Notes: Leadership/Licensure. Denver, CO: Education Commission of the States.

Billot, J. (2003). The real and the ideal: The role and workload of secondary principals in New Zealand. *International Studies in Educational Administration, 31*(1), 33–49.

Bottoms, G., & O'Neill, K. (2001). *SREB - Preparing a new breed of school principals: It's time for action.* Atlanta, GA: Southern Regional Education Board.

Bottoms, G., O'Neill, K., Fry, B., & Hill, D. (2003). *Good principals are the key to successful schools: Six strategies to prepare more good principals.* Atlanta, GA: Southern Regional Education Board.

Brimm, J. (1983). What stresses school administrators. *Theory Into Practice, 22*(1), 64–70.

Broad Foundation & Thomas B. Fordham Institute. (2003). *Better leaders for America's schools: A manifesto.* Los Angeles: Authors.

Cave, E., & Wilkinson, C. (1992). Developing managerial capabilities in education. In N. Bennett, M. Crawford, & C. Riches (Eds.), *Managing change in education: Individual and organizational perspectives* (pp. 34–45). London: Chapman.

Chen, P. Y., & Popovich, P. M. (2002). *Correlation: Parametric and nonparametric measures* (Sage University Papers Series on Quantitative Applications in the Social Sciences, 07-139). Thousand Oaks, CA: Sage.

Cochran-Smith, M. (2005). The politics of teacher education and the curse of complexity. *Journal of Teacher Education, 56*(3), 181–185.

Cohen, J., & Cohen, P. (1983). *Applied multiple regression/correlation analysis for the behavioral sciences* (2nd ed.). Hillsdale, NJ: Erlbaum.

Copland, M. A. (2000). Problem-based learning and prospective principals' problem-framing ability. *Educational Administration Quarterly, 36*, 585–607.

Council of Chief State School Officers. (2007). *Key state education policies on K–12 education: 2006.* Washington, DC: Author.

Daniel, K. B., Kyle, J. E., & Ulrich, D. W. (2005). Identifying gaps in secondary principals' knowledge and skills. *Dissertation Abstracts International, 67*(03), 790A. (UMI No. 3211606)

Daresh, J. C. (1986). Support for beginning principals: First hurdles are highest. *Theory Into Practice, 25*(3), 168–173.

Daresh, J. C. (2006). *Beginning the principalship: A practical guide for new leaders.* Thousand Oaks, CA: Corwin Press.

Daresh, J. C., & Male, T. (2000). Crossing the border into leadership: Experiences of newly appointed British headteachers and American principals. *Educational Management and Administration, 28,* 89–101.

Daresh, J. C., & Playko, M. A. (1989, October). *In search of critical skills for beginning principals.* Paper presented at the annual meeting of the University Council for Educational Administration, Phoenix, AZ. (ERIC Document Reproduction Service No. ED311548)

Daresh, J. C., & Playko, M. A. (1992, April). *What do beginning leaders need?: Aspiring and practicing principals' perceptions of critical skills for novice administrators.* Paper presented at the annual meeting of the American Educational Research Association, San Francisco. (ERIC Document Reproduction Service No. ED344312)

Daresh, J. C, & Playko, M. A. (1993, October). *Leadership focusing on the needs of learners: Probability or empty hope for new principals?* Paper presented at the annual meeting of the University Council for Educational Administration, Houston, TX. (ERIC Document Reproduction Service No. ED362678)

Datnow, A., & Castellano, M. E. (2001). Managing and guiding school reform: Leadership in success for all schools. *Educational Administration Quarterly, 37*(2), 219–249.

Davis, S., Darling-Hammond, L., LaPointe, M., & Meyerson, D. (2005). *School leadership study: Developing successful principals.* Stanford, CA: Stanford Educational Leadership Institute and Wallace Foundation.

Duke, D. L. (1987). *School leadership and instructional improvement.* New York: Random House.

Dunning, G. (1996). Management problems of new primary headteachers. *School Organisation, 16*(1), 111–128.

Elmore, R. F. (2003). *Knowing the right thing to do: School improvement and performance-based accountability.* Washington, DC: National Governors Association.

Elmore, R. F. (2007). Education: A "profession" in search of practice. *Teaching in Educational Administration, 15*(1), 1–4.

Farkas, S., Johnson, J., & Duffett, A. (2004). *Rolling up their sleeves: Superintendents and principals talk about what's needed to fix public schools.* Pleasantville, NY: Public Agenda/ DeWitt Wallace and Reader's Digest Fund.

Farkas, S., Johnson, J., Duffett, A., & Foleno, T. (2001). *Trying to stay ahead of the game: Superintendents and principals talk about school leadership.* Pleasantville, NY: Public Agenda/DeWitt Wallace and Reader's Digest Fund.

Feistritzer, E. (2003). *Certification of public-school administrators.* Washington, DC: National Center for Education Information.

Gates, S. M., Ringel, J. S., & Santibanez, L. (2003). *Who is leading our schools?: An overview of school administrators and their careers.* Santa Monica, CA: RAND.

Goldring, E., & Rallis, S. F. (1993). *Principals of dynamic schools: Taking charge of change.* Newbury Park, CA: Corwin Press.

Greenfield, W. D. (1995). Toward a theory of school administration: The centrality of leadership. *Educational Administration Quarterly, 31,* 61–85.

Hale, E. L., & Moorman, H. N. (2003, September). *Preparing school principals: A national perspective on policy and program innovations.* Washington, DC: Institute for Educational Leadership and Illinois Education Research Council.

Hallinger, P., & Heck, R. H. (1996). Reassessing the principal's role in school effectiveness: A review of empirical research 1980–1995. *Educational Administration Quarterly, 32*, 5–43.

Hallinger, P., & McCary, C. E. (1990). Developing the strategic thinking of instructional leaders. *Elementary School Journal, 91*, 89–108.

Heck, R. H., & Hallinger, P. (1999). Next generation methods for the study of leadership and school improvement. In J. Murphy & K. S. Louis (Eds.), *Handbook of educational administration* (2nd ed., pp. 141–162). San Francisco: Jossey-Bass.

Heck, R. H., & Hallinger, P. (2005). The study of educational leadership and management: Where does the field stand today? *Educational Management Administration and Leadership, 33*(2), 229–244.

Herr, N. J. (2002). Addressing shortages in the principalship: Perceptions of novice administrators in Pennsylvania. *Dissertation Abstracts International, 64*(07), 2326A. (UMI No. 3097229)

Herrington, C. D., & Wills, B. K. (2005). Decertifying the principalship: The politics of administrator preparation in Florida. *Educational Policy, 19*(1), 181–200.

Hess, F. M. (2003). A license to lead? A new leadership agenda for America's schools. In *21st century schools project* (pp. 1–24). Washington, DC: Progressive Policy Institute.

Howell, B. (1981). Profile of the principalship. *Educational Leadership, 38*, 333–337.

Institute for Educational Leadership. (2000). *Leadership for student learning: Reinventing the principalship.* Washington, DC: Author.

Jackson, B. L., & Kelley, C. (2002). Exceptional and innovative programs in educational leadership. *Educational Administration Quarterly, 38*, 192–212.

Kerrins, J. A. (2001). Take this job and fill it. *Leadership, 30*(5), 20–24.

Kowalski, T. J. (2004). The ongoing war for the soul of school administration. In T. J. Lasley (Ed.), *Better leaders for America's schools: Perspectives on the Manifesto* (pp. 92–114). Columbia, MO: University Council for Educational Administration.

Kowalski, T. J. (2008). Preparing and licensing superintendents in three contiguous states. *Planning and Changing, 39*, 240–260.

Kowalski, T. J. (2009). Need to address evidence-based practice in educational administration. *Educational Administration Quarterly, 45*, 375–423.

Kowalski, T. J. (2010). *The school principal: Visionary leadership and competent management.* New York: Routledge.

Kowalski, T. J., Place, A. W., Edmister, J., & Zigler, T. (2009). Need for practice-based research in school administration. *Mid-Western Educational Researcher. 22*(4), 2–8.

Kruger, M. L., van Eck, E., & Vermeulen, A. (2005). Why principals leave: Risk factors for premature departure in the Netherlands compared for women and men. *School Leadership and Management, 25*, 241–261.

Larson, M. S. (1977). *The rise of professionalism: A sociological analysis.* Berkeley: University of California Press.

Leithwood, K., & Jantzi, D. (2000). Principal and teacher leadership effects: A replication. *School Leadership and Management, 20,* 415–434.

Leithwood K., & Riehl, C. (2003, March). *What do we already know about successful school leadership.* Paper prepared for the AERA Division A Task Force on Developing Research in Educational Leadership, Chicago.

Leithwood, K., & Stager, M. (1986, April). *Differences in how moderately and highly effective principals classify and manage their problems.* Paper presented at the annual conference of the American Educational Research Association, San Francisco.

Levin, H. M. (2006). Can research improve educational leadership? *Educational Researcher, 35*(8), 38–43.

Loder, T. L., & Spillane, J. P. (2005). Is a principal still a teacher?: US women administrators' accounts of role conflict and role discontinuity. *School Leadership and Management, 25,* 263–279.

Lyons, J. E. (1999, Winter). How school principals perceive their roles, rewards, and challenges. *ERS Spectrum,* pp. 18–23.

Marks, H. M., & Printy, S. M. (2003). Principal leadership and school performance: An integration of transformational and instructional leadership. *Educational Administration Quarterly, 39,* 370–397.

May, W. F. (2001). *Beleaguered rulers: The public obligation of the professional.* Louisville, KY: Westminster John Knox Press.

McGuire, M. Y. (2002). *Elevating educational leadership task force report.* Report issued by the Michigan Board of Education. Lansing, MI: Michigan Department of Education.

Milstein, M. M., & Krueger, J. A. (1997). Improving educational administration preparation programs: What we have learned over the past decade. *Peabody Journal of Education, 72*(2), 100–116.

Murphy, J. (2002). Reculturing the profession of educational leadership: New blueprints. *Educational Administration Quarterly, 38,* 176–191.

Murphy, J. (2003, September). *Reculturing educational leadership: The ISLLC standards ten years out.* Paper prepared for the National Board of Educational Administration.

Muse, I. D., & Thomas, G. A. (1991). The thinning ranks of rural school administration: The principalship in trouble. *Rural Educator, 13*(1), 8–12. (ERIC Document Reproduction Service No. EJ436556)

National Association of Elementary School Principals. (1979). *The elementary school principalship in 1978: A research study.* Arlington, VA: Author.

National Association of Secondary School Principals. (2001). *Priorities and barriers in high school leadership: A survey of principals.* Reston, VA: Author.

National Center for Education Statistics. (1997). *Public and private school principals in the United States: A statistical profile 1987–88 to 1993–94* (U.S. Department of Education Publication No. NCES 97-455). Washington, DC: U.S. Government Printing Office.

National Center for Education Statistics. (2007). *Condition of education.* Washington, DC: Author.

Oancea, A., & Furlong, J. (2007). Expressions of excellence and the assessment of applied and practice-based research. *Research Papers in Education, 22*(2), 119–137.

Ohio Department of Education. (2005, June). *Condition of teacher supply and demand in Ohio: A data summary for the Ohio State Board of Education.* Columbus, OH: Author.

Ohio Department of Education. (2006). *Ohio standards for principals.* Columbus, OH: Author.

Ortiz, F. I. (1982). *Career patterns in education: Men, women, and minorities in public school administration.* New York: Praeger.

Ozga, J. (1993). *Women in educational management.* Milton Keynes, UK: Open University Press.

Parkay, F. W., Currie, G. D., & Rhodes, J. W. (1992). Professional socialization: A longitudinal study of first-time high school principals. *Educational Administration Quarterly, 28*, 43–75.

Parkay, F. W., & Hall, G. E. (1992). *Becoming a principal: The challenges of beginning leadership.* Boston: Allyn & Bacon.

Peterson, K. D. (2002). The professional development of principals: Innovations and opportunities. *Educational Administration Quarterly, 38*, 212–232.

Peterson, K., Murphy. J., & Hallinger, P. (1987). Superintendents' perceptions of the control and coordination of technical care in effective school districts. *Educational Administration Quarterly, 23*, 79–95.

Portin, B. S., & Shen, J. (1998). The changing principalship: Its current status, variability, and impact. *Journal of Leadership Studies, 5*(3), 93–113.

Quong, T. (2006). Asking the hard questions: Being a beginning principal in Australia. *Journal of Educational Administration, 44*(4), 376–388.

Reynolds, D. (2002). *Final report (2002).* Nottingham, UK: National College for School Leadership.

Rodriguez-Campos, L., Rincones-Gomez, R., & Shen, J. (2005). Secondary principals' educational attainment, experience, and professional development in the USA. *International Journal of Leadership in Education, 8*, 309–319.

Ruhl-Smith, C. D., Shen, J., & Cooley, V. E. (1999). Gender differences in reasons for entering and leaving education administration: Discriminant function analyses. *Journal of Psychology, 133*, 596–604.

Rutherford, W. L., Hord, S. M., & Thurber, J. C. (1984). Preparing principals for leadership roles in school improvement. *Education and Urban Society, 17*, 29–48.

Shakeshaft, C. (1999). The struggle to create a more gender-inclusive profession. In J. Murphy & K. Louis (Eds.), *Handbook of research on educational administration* (pp. 99–118). San Francisco: Jossey-Bass.

Shen, J., Cooley, V. E., & Wegenke, G. L. (2004). Perspectives on factors influencing application for the principalship: A comparative study of teachers, principals and superintendents. *International Journal of Leadership in Education, 7*, 57–70.

Thompson, M. A., & Legler, R. (2003, August). Principalship in the Midwest: The role of principal preparation programs. *North Central Regional Educational Laboratory Policy Issues, 14*, 1–11.

Tredway, L., Brill, F., & Hernandez, J. (2007). Taking off the cape: The stories of novice urban leadership. *Theory Into Practice, 46*(3), 212–221.

VanderJagt, D., Shen, J., & Hsieh, C. (2001). Elementary and secondary public school principals' perceptions of school problems. *Educational Research Quarterly, 25*, 39–51.

Walker, K., & Carr-Stewart, S. (2006). Beginning principals: Experiences and images of success. *International Studies in Educational Administration, 34*(3), 17–36.

Walker, E., Mitchell, C., & Turner, W. (1999, April). *Professional development and urban leadership: A study of urban administrators' perceptions of what matters most in their professional development.* Paper presented at the annual meeting of the American Educational Research Association, Montreal, Quebec, Canada. (ERIC Document Reproduction Service No. ED431826)

Waters, T., & Grubb, S. (2004). *The leadership we need: Using research to strengthen the use of standards for administrator preparation and licensure programs.* Denver, CO: Mid-continent Research for Education and Learning.

Waters, T., Marzano, R., & McNulty, B. (2003). *Balanced leadership: What 30 years of research tells about the effect of leadership on student achievement.* Denver, CO: Mid-continent Research for Education and Learning.

Yerkes, D. M., & Guaglianone, C. L. (1998). Where have all the high school administrators gone? *Thrust for Educational Leadership, 28*(2), 10–14.

Young, M., Peterson, G., & Short, P. (2002). The complexity of substantive reform: A call for interdependence among key stakeholders. *Educational Administration Quarterly, 38*, 187–175.

CHAPTER 5

ACCELERATING NEW PRINCIPAL DEVELOPMENT THROUGH LEADERSHIP COACHING

Chad R. Lochmiller and Michael Silver

New principals face a rush of expectations beginning from their first day on the job and often find themselves left alone to deal with these challenges. Induction support is rarely guaranteed in most districts and support from their university-based preparation program is often not available once a principal completes or graduates from their preparation program. Given the challenges facing new principals, it is easy to understand how new principals are distracted from the core work of improving teaching and learning and overwhelmed by the demands of school leadership. Consider this first-year principal's experience:

> When I started out at this school, I found a ton of things to do. There were human resource issues that had not been addressed. There were instructional issues that the previous principal had not attended to. I had to hire a new office manager; there were teacher positions that weren't filled. Student behavior was terrible. The school was just a total mess....

The Challenges for New Principals in the Twenty-First Century:
Developing Leadership Capabilities Through Professional Support, pp. 101–120
Copyright © 2010 by Information Age Publishing

I felt like my preparation program prepared me for the high-level things that principals do. It talked about visioning, instructional leadership, and other things. But when I started it was a huge shock because it was about doing. I realized really quickly what I didn't know. I learned a ton about that. And—I learned that this wasn't going to be easy. The school would need a lot more than I knew how to provide.

Research increasingly suggests that new principals, much like the one quoted, benefit from formal induction (Spiro, Mattis, & Mitgang, 2007). There has been a steady increase in the number of induction programs for school principals in the past decade (Hall, 2008; Malone, 2001). A variety of induction models have been proposed by researchers and practitioners (Anderson, 1991; Bloom, Castagna, Moir, & Warren, 2005; Reiss, 2007; Villani, 2006). Leadership coaching, or "the practice of providing deliberate support to another individual to help him/her to clarify and/or to achieve goals" (Bloom et al., 2005, p. 5), has become an especially common form of induction for new school principals. The primary purpose of coaching is to accelerate learning, ease entry into professional roles through socialization, and focus support on individual strengths. While leadership coaching has become a popular form of support for new principals, its impact on principals' leadership practice—particularly instructional leadership—is unclear.

In this chapter, we discuss research conducted in a university-based leadership coaching program. The program provides leadership coaching support to newly certified school principals who complete a traditional university-based principal preparation program. The leadership coaching program we studied is working to improve the induction experience for new principals in school districts located throughout the region. Two research questions guide our study. First, what are the challenges that new principals face? Second, how do leadership coaches support new principals? The study describes how leadership coaches are using a model of leadership coaching developed by the program and explores the impact that this model appears to have on the principal's leadership practice. The chapter unfolds with a brief discussion of literature. Following our review of literature, we discuss the program and the coaching model used by the program's leadership coaches. Following a discussion of the research methods, we then discuss the results we obtained from our analysis. We conclude by discussing our findings and their implications for supporting new school principals.

REVIEW OF LITERATURE

Evidence increasingly suggests that school districts are experiencing difficulty finding qualified school principals for open administrative positions

(Gates et al., 2006; Roza, Celio, Harvey, & Wilson, 2003). Additionally, school districts are facing substantial turnover among experienced principals as the principal workforce approaches retirement age (Papa & Baxter, 2005; Pounder, Galvin, & Shepherd, 2003). These challenges are especially pronounced in urban centers and at the high school level (Papa & Baxter, 2005). Moreover, principals indicate that increasing accountability pressures, expanding responsibility, the elimination of tenure, and inadequate compensation are among the key factors driving them out of the principalship (Whitaker, 2002). The combination of these challenges makes providing support for all principals—but particularly new principals—more important than at any previous time.

New principals need induction support that helps them become familiar with the principalship and that helps them learn to manage conditions that influence their leadership. States have only recently begun to require districts to provide induction support (Spiro et al., 2007). Whether new principals have access to induction support currently depends on the existence of a formal or informal district mentoring program. Many districts throughout the United States provide an informal mentor for new principals. These ad hoc relationships rarely extend beyond the principal's first year and typically focus on district operating procedures or administrative culture as opposed to instructional leadership (Malone, 2001). The tenuous nature of support for new principals makes their first few years on the job a competition for survival (Bloom et al., 2005).

Viewing principal induction as a socialization process helps explain why induction matters (Daresh, 2004). When viewed as a socialization process, induction becomes the first few steps on a principal's path toward professional self-sufficiency, which are then continued through other professional learning opportunities throughout the principal's career. Daresh (2004) suggested that the socialization process begins when a principal starts working in a full-time position. Socialization may include individuals within the school from whom the principal acquires guidance, direction, or support (Barnett, 1995; Crow & Matthews, 1998; Daresh, 2004). Lortie (2009) points out that principals undergo considerable work socialization in their prior regular positions as teachers. Hart (1993) also suggested that the professional socialization of new principals may begin as early as teaching, but is also influenced by principal preparation programs. Several studies on the socialization of principals and heads of schools identified phases or stages to understand principal socialization and capture experiences prior to working as principals. For example, Ribbins (1998) names two phases in the early socialization of school heads as "formation" and "accession," and Reeves, Moos, and Forrest (1998) describe a "warm-up" or "pre-entry" stage as the first of eight stages in socialization of head teachers before entry as a head. In addition,

Weindling (2000) introduces a model of stages of transition through the headship role and describes early experiences of heads in their preparation.

Regardless of the starting point, research connecting socialization theory and induction suggests that induction creates an opportunity for new principals to become familiar with and comfortable in their role. It is a process that helps new administrators learn the requisite knowledge, skills, behaviors, and values to take on complex, responsibility-laden school leadership roles (Crow & Matthews, 1998). Parkay, Currie, and Rhodes (1992) concluded that these initial experiences may significantly influence a principal's future performance as a leader.

Given the importance of support for new principals, several researchers have advocated for the creation of "a structured, systematic process for learning how to deal effectively with various school-specific problems" (p. 59). Principals cannot and should not be left alone to figure out complex school problems. Despite the logic of this argument, Schainker and Roberts (1987) identified a surprising paradox between research and practice. While research generally acknowledges that a principal's most valuable source of learning is their on-the-job experience, practice provides principals few opportunities to engage in this learning in the course of their regular work. Indeed, recent research suggests that an absence of effective support for principals may be contributing to the exodus of principals (Whitaker, 2002).

The leadership coaching process is the kind of structural support for principals emphasized in this study. Leadership coaching is more intentional in the level of support and methods used for structuring interactions between the coach and new administrator. Bloom and colleagues (2005) describe a coach as one who "provides continuing support that is safe and confidential and has as its goal the nurturing of significant personal, professional, and institutional growth through a process that unfolds over time" (p. 10). Effective coaching relationships require trust, confidentiality, and professional rapport between the coach and the coachee. Furthermore, effective coaching requires that coach and coachee establish a shared understanding of coaching. This requires conceptualizing the role of a coach as someone who (1) sees what others may not see through the quality of his or her attention or listening, (2) is in the position to step back (or invite participants to step back) from the situation so that they have enough distance from it to get some perspective, (3) helps people see the difference between their intentions and their thinking or actions, and (4) helps people cut through patterns of illusion and self-deception caused by defensive thinking and behavior (Hargrove, 1995).

As the principalship has increasingly become focused on instructional leadership, the need for induction that prepares, supports, and assists principals in serving as instructional leaders has also increased. Researchers have long argued that principals must be instructional leaders in order to have the greatest impact on schools (Rowan, 1995; Spillane, Halverson, & Diamond, 2001). Stein and Nelson (2003) asserted that principals must "know strong instruction when they see it, to encourage it when they don't, and to set the conditions for continuous academic learning among their professional staffs" (p. 424). To do so effectively, principals must engage in an influence relationship that motivates, enables, and supports teachers' efforts to learn about and change their instructional practices (Spillane, Hallet, & Diamond, 2003). While leadership coaching is a method of supporting new principals, the connection between leadership coaching and instructional leadership remains unclear.

RESEARCH DESIGN

Using a case study research design, we studied the support provided to new principals participating in a university-based leadership coaching program (Creswell, 1998; Merriam, 1998). We adopted a purposeful sampling strategy to select participants for this study. We selected participants in the program that wielded the greatest contrast between principals, coaches, and coaching pairs (Miles & Huberman, 1994). The sample reflected different school levels, contexts, and learning improvement challenges. We conducted repeated interviews with program participants as well as regular observations of program activities (Patton, 2002). We used an interview and observation guide to guide the collection of data as well as ensure that the data collected supported the research questions for the study. The interview protocols were focused on the coaching process, including the types of questions asked by the coach as well as the follow-through demonstrated by the coachee. We also collected documents and other artifacts from the program. Of particular value, we collected coaching logs prepared by the leadership coaches during their coaching sessions. The logs formed a record of the coaching relationship over time.

SAMPLE

Our study included 50 interviews conducted with 30 program participants. The composition of the sample was limited to those administrators who graduated from the university or who participated in the program on a fee-for-service basis. Of the participants we interviewed, 12 graduated from the university's educational administration program; four were participating in the program on a fee-for-service basis; 12 were leadership coaches assigned to the school administrator; and 2 were program staff.

The sample included nine elementary school principals, four middle school principals, and three high school principals. The sample included 12 female administrators and 4 male administrators. All of the administrators were Caucasian. Four male leadership coaches and eight female leadership coaches also participated in this study. The program employed eight Caucasian leadership coaches, three African American coaches, and one Asian American leadership coach.

The schools were primarily located in suburban districts in the Pacific Northwest. The schools served primarily low- to middle-income families. The elementary schools ranged in size from 250 to 400 students. On average, 71% of the school's students qualified for free lunch, 14% were students of color, and 7% were English language learners. At the middle and high school level, the schools ranged in size from 800 to 1,650 students. On average, 43% of the school's students qualified for free or reduced-price lunch, 12% were students of color, and 4% were English language learners. Eight of the elementary schools and one of the middle schools were eligible for Title I. One of the high schools had been converted into a school-within-a-school model, whereby each unit is a smaller school. The remaining high schools were traditional comprehensive high schools.

DATA ANALYSIS

Interviews, observations, and documents were coded using an open-coding scheme. Our coding scheme utilized a combination of descriptive, interpretive, and pattern codes. We applied descriptive codes to passages of text, which described the characteristics of the participants or their school, the challenges they faced, or the conditions surrounding their leadership. We applied interpretive codes to passages of text, which were related to our conceptual framework (see the purposeful coaching model below). Finally, we applied pattern codes for those actions and activities, which constituted basic behaviors of the purposeful coaching model. The coding scheme was constructed to reflect research questions, a strategy described in detail by Miles and Huberman (1994, pp. 56–65). In coding transcripts and documents collected throughout the study, we looked for passages of text that identified challenges raised by the new principals, the support provided by the leadership coaches, and the perceived impact that this support had on the principal's instructional leadership. We especially sought examples from the coaches' experience that described an administrator's struggles or challenges and what they (the coach) did to support them. Coaching logs were analyzed using the same coding approach. In total, the study included more than 50 interviews, nearly 200 hours of nonparticipant observation, and more than 320 documents and artifacts, including nearly 250 coaching logs.

DESCRIPTION OF THE UNIVERSITY-BASED COACHING PROGRAM AND COACHING MODEL STUDIED

The leadership coaching program we studied is housed at a private, mid-sized university in the western United States. The university's educational administration program began providing coaching support to graduates of the principal certification program in 2006. The program provides support at no charge to any graduate who secures a full-time administrative position for a period of 3 years. In the first and second years of coaching support, the administrator and the leadership coach meet 4–6 hours per month. The frequency and length of the meetings decreases in the third year. Coaches receive a small stipend for each administrator coached. The program serves approximately 15 graduates of the university. In addition, the program provides coaching support to administrators in local school districts on a fee-for-service basis. In total, the program serves more than 50 school administrators, including those in two of the state's largest school systems. The program employs approximately 30 leadership coaches.

Retired school and district administrators serve as leadership coaches in the program. The program recruits coaches from school districts by word of mouth and uses an application process. The coaches participate in ongoing training focused on different aspects of coaching and strategies for working with new administrators. The program requires leadership coaches to complete coaching logs during each coaching session. These logs document the challenges, successes, and next steps that each coach and coachee discuss. The coach submits the logs to the program director. Additionally, leadership coaches are observed by the program director twice a year.

THE PURPOSEFUL COACHING MODEL

The program has developed a unique model of leadership coaching, which is referred to as the purposeful coaching model (PCM). The model is specifically focused on helping new principals develop the skills needed to improve instructional practice in their buildings. Unlike other models advanced in the educational leadership field, this model is primarily concerned with accelerating principals' development to engage in instructional leadership. The purpose of purposeful coaching is to promote improved instructional practice and, thereby, improve student achievement. The PCM is based on prior research on blended coaching

(Bloom et al., 2005) as well as research from the business field on evidence-based coaching (Strober & Grant, 2006). It also draws from research on action research, a methodology that connects research, reflection, and practice (Stringer, 2003; Winter, Burroughs, & Burroughs, 1989). Borrowing from Hargrove (1995), the model assumes that leadership coaches provide support to new principals by gathering evidence, asking questions, managing reflection, and monitoring action. In short, leadership coaches become a second set of eyes to help principals understand, interpret, and respond to the leadership challenges in their schools. Figure 5.1 illustrates the central aspects of the PCM. As illustrated, leadership coaches interact with the new principals and gather evidence, ask questions, manage reflection, and monitor principals' actions in order to ensure that they remain focused on teaching and learning. These strategies are intentional and meant to help new principals understand the challenges for learning improvement as well as clarify thinking about teaching and learning. More specifically, the coaches help new principals identify the assumptions they are making about learning improvement.

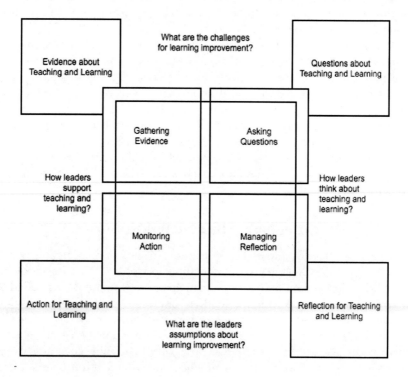

Figure 5.1.   Purposeful coaching model.

The primary purpose of the coaching model is to link leadership coaching to the principal's role as an instructional leader and leader of learning improvement.

RESEARCH FINDINGS

We began our analysis by analyzing entries on coaching logs. We analyzed these logs to determine the challenges that new principals reported to their leadership coaches. The logs were submitted by leadership coaches over a 2-year period and describe the specific issues, challenges, or concerns new principals had throughout the coaching relationship. Our analysis reveals that principals faced a number of challenges related to classroom instruction. The frequency with which these issues were listed on the coaching logs indicates that they consumed a majority of the new principal's time and were a common topic in the coaching sessions.

Table 5.1 illustrates the 10 most frequently cited challenges on the coaching logs we analyzed. Based on more than 800 entries on more than 200 coaching logs, we found that 6 of the 10 most frequently reported challenges were related to classroom instruction or instructional improvement. The top three challenges recorded on the coaching logs related to observing classroom instruction, conducting learning walks, and writing effective teacher evaluations. Taken together, nearly half of the references on the coaching logs we analyzed related to instruction, or the principal's role as an instructional leader.

Table 5.1.   Challenges Facing New Principals

Challenges Reported by New Principals	Rank	% of Total Reference
Observing classroom instruction	1	21%
Conducting learning walks	2	15%
Writing teacher evaluations	3	13%
Relationship or trust building with staff	4	12%
Planning professional development for teachers	5	10%
Planning for school improvement	6	8%
Creating professional learning communities	7	7%
Communicating with teachers and staff	8	5%
Addressing diversity or equity issues	9	1%
Managing time or workload	10	1%

Percentage represents frequency as reflected as a percentage of 807 total references/does not add to 100%

To understand why these issues were so prevalent, we interviewed leadership coaches and the new principals they support. The interviews revealed that the new principals saw instructional issues as being especially complicated. The coaches indicate that the new principals had to learn a variety of skills in order to successfully impact or address instructional practice. The coaches' statements indicate that this was especially true for issues related to teacher performance. Principals needed to not only have a well-formed understanding of effective instruction but also the capacity to offer meaningful feedback to classroom teachers about their instructional practice.

The interviews we conducted with coaches and the new principals they worked with offered several poignant examples of the challenges facing new principals. In one example, an elementary principal was appointed to a school that had several lingering personnel issues that the previous principal had not resolved. Of particular concern, the principal had to move a teacher from a plan of improvement into the formal dismissal process. This required that she not only understand what had been done previously but what needed to be done. Her leadership coach explained the situation:

> The principal I'm working with inherited some issues that most new principals don't have to face.... She inherited a school that basically had no direction ... and that had some very serious teacher performance issues that the previous principal did not deal with. Most of her time has been focused on a few teachers ... one, in particular, because the teacher has to be removed and she is having to learn about all of the human resource processes that have to be done to remove the teacher.... We've spent a lot of time on that. Because so much of her time is focused on this teacher she can't get time to do other observations, to plan professional development, or to really be out in front of the staff promoting her vision for the school.... She's trapped in the forms and processes. You really do have to learn the process by doing it. I think that's the only way. After you've done it once or twice, then it becomes easier.

As this comment suggests, the new principal was unprepared for the process of removing a classroom teacher and therefore had to learn the process as she completed it. As the principal explained:

> I did not understand how much work it would be to remove a teacher or to try to focus on improving instructional practice.... As a classroom teacher, I don't think I ever thought about it. I mean, I understand my classroom and my students, but I never saw what it took on the principal's side. When I became principal here, I was given a pretty hard case to deal with.... I had to figure out what the previous principal did and what I needed to do to make sure that there was no break in the process. I had to learn about doing

learning-walks and formal observations, I had to learn what to say on the evaluation and observation form.... This one teacher has become my sole focus because the process is so complicated and the things that I have to do are so detailed.

GATHERING EVIDENCE, ASKING QUESTIONS, AND MANAGING REFLECTION

Given the complexity of the challenges facing new principals, we sought to understand how coaches used the PCM advanced by the program to provide support for the new principals they worked with. Our analysis of coaching logs, interview transcripts, and observation notes reveals that leadership coaches provided substantial support for the new principals by gathering evidence about the new principals' practice or the schools' needs, asking them questions about their leadership action or the conditions they identified, and helping the new principals reflect on their leadership practice. Each of these activities appeared to help new principals focus their leadership action on key learning improvement challenges in their schools.

The coaches employed a variety of strategies to gather evidence, which they could later use to help new principals focus their leadership actions. We found two approaches especially compelling. In one case, a leadership coach videotaped a principal leading a staff meeting and then used the video as the basis for her coaching session to help the principal see where he missed opportunities to focus on instructional issues and student learning. In the second case, a coach conducted short teacher focus groups using a modified "360-degree" evaluation with staff in the principal's building. He used the results of the focus group to help the new principal see where his leadership practice was having more or less impact on classroom teachers.

Videotaping Principals' Leadership Practice

As one coach noted, "My coaching has to focus on the principal's practice and so there is a need for me to collect information about them as a leader, their staff, students, and their schools." In this instance, the coach videotaped the principal leading a staff meeting that was focused on creating professional learning communities in each department in his high school. The coach used the tape as the focus for her next coaching session with the principal. The coach began her coaching by asking, "What did you do or could you have done to focus on student achievement in this meeting?" The coachee, who was a high school principal, replied by describing his thinking and then the places where he believed he could have been more acutely focused on issues related to students. For example, after watching the video, he noted that he made few references to student achievement data, focused on operational issues, and tended to focus on issues about "making it work" as opposed to "making it good." As the principal commented in a follow-up interview,

> the video helped me see where I was missing opportunities to make references to students and to student achievement.... As I went into the next week, I worked with [the coach] to plan an agenda that would lend itself to some opportunities to have the conversation be more about achievement and instructional practice.... My plan was to open with data from a recent staff and student survey, then link it to our student achievement concerns, and then move into describing the shape of the professional learning communities.... So, instead of leaping into the PLC conversation, I created some space in the meeting to talk about why it mattered and how it connected.

Teacher Focus Groups

As an alternative strategy, a leadership coach conducted focus groups with classroom teachers in a new principal's school and used the data he gathered from these focus groups to inform his coaching of the new principal. The coach referred to these focus groups as a modified "360-degree evaluation" with the purpose being to help the new principal "calibrate" what he thought he was doing as a leader with what his staff said they saw him doing. Unlike the coach who videotaped the principal in order to determine how the principal's leadership practice was *delivered*, this coach used the teacher focus groups to understand how the principal's leadership was *received* by the staff.

The focus groups were composed of staff members whom the principal selected and ranged from those who supported his efforts to those who had shown some reservations or resistance. Based on the comments offered by the teachers, the coach used the group to gauge the nature of the relationship that the principal had established with the teachers as well as to determine how well the teachers understood where the principal was trying to take the school. "I use the evaluation as a way to check the temperature of the school ... to see if the principal is making a connection with staff ... to see if the principal is talking consistently and keeping his vision in front."

Based on the evidence the coach collected through the focus group, it appeared to the coach that the principal needed to attend to some issues related to how he communicated with staff and make his expectations clear. The new principal indicated that this feedback was particularly helpful. The feedback "acted like a mirror.... It showed me where I needed to improve and it also showed my teachers that I was serious about improving my relationships with them. I couldn't get that feedback without the coach interviewing them." In response, the principal looked more closely at how he was communicating with staff before, during, and after formal classroom observations as well as exploring ways that he could communicate with the staff more frequently about what he saw as the key steps for the goal. The principal noted that "I ended up changing how I debriefed observations with the classroom teachers and what kind of feedback I provided to them."

Both examples illustrate how the coaches used the PCM to gather evidence about the principal's leadership practice and their schools in order to inform their coaching as well as to focus the principal they worked with on aspects of their leadership that either required attention or were not as effective as the principal might have perceived. As one of the coaches commented later, "Reflection is really like the bridge between what we're seeing and what they need to see in order for them to address it." Asked why the combination of evidence, questions, and reflection were so important, the coaches generally acknowledged that the purpose of coaching using this model was to help the new principal develop an instructional routine.

HELPING NEW PRINCIPALS DEVELOP AN INSTRUCTIONAL ROUTINE

Using the evidence they collected, a variety of questions, and by helping the new principals reflect, the leadership coaches helped the new principals develop what one coach referred to as an "instructional routine." The instructional routine described how the new principals addressed priorities or challenges related to classroom instruction. The instructional routine broadly described the work of instructional leadership. Asked what an instructional routine involved, a coach replied:

> What I am referring to is how they lead instruction.... What they do on a regular basis to improve teaching and learning. I am referring to the way that they conduct observations, learning walks, write evaluations, and talk to teachers about their instruction.... I refer to that as a routine because it needs to be done every single day.

Interviews with coaches revealed that they often participated with the principals in developing their instructional routines. In several cases, the coach and new principal conducted a walk-through in each of their coaching sessions. In another case, the coach and new principal developed a rubric to help teachers reach a common definition of instructional rigor in advance of implementing a new instructional program. The coaches took the development of these routines seriously and often devoted considerable time to them. As one of the coaches noted in her interview, "for me coaching is all about classroom instruction and what the principal does to support the teacher in their work to provide powerful instruction for children."

Several of the principals who were receiving coaching support indicated that their leadership coaches were particularly helpful in developing effective teacher evaluations and providing constructive feedback to classroom teachers on their instructional practice. This appeared to be an important focus for the leadership coaches we studied and an especially important aspect of their instructional routine. Several of the new principals acknowledged that "it's never easy to critique someone's teaching." Other principals described their initial interactions with classroom teachers as "uncertain," "uneasy," "afraid," and "awkward." Principals reported that their leadership coach helped them prepare for these conversations. Coaches indicated that this was one of the most important aspects of their work as it connected directly with classroom instruction and, therefore, had the most direct impact on student learning. Coaches generally acknowledged that the new principals they worked with ranged in their ability to observe instruction and provide effective feedback aimed at improving instruction.

Several coaches indicated that new principals they were working with were often unsure about what good or effective instruction looked like and that this was an especially important focus for their coaching support. As one coach stated very eloquently, "Principals have experience as the instructor but not the leader of instruction.... When they go into the classroom, they have to learn to overcome their experience as a classroom teacher." This coach was particularly clear that this was an area where her coachee was struggling. As she suggested:

> I'm not sure [my coachee] really knows what he is looking at when he looks at teaching and learning. I'm not sure he understands how the results of classroom assessment should be used to drive instruction or how that's managed. I'm not clear that he gets how to do professional development within the classroom setting as well as external to it.... I think he's not yet clear about his role when he goes into a classroom. He needs to be interacting with students, looking at work, etc. But I think he tends to be unsure how to do that.

The coach explained that she had recently completed a classroom observation with the coachee and found that he was "hesitant to get into the room and really see what was happening." The coach recalled that she entered the room and immediately interacted with students, asking them questions and engaging with them to determine how well they understood the instructional goals. In contrast, the principal sat down and did not interact. In his own interview, the coachee recalled that observation and noted, "I still have that thing inside my head where I don't want to be in the teacher's way so I tend to be more the fly on the wall." As the coach later reflected, "He needs to overcome his past experience.... He needs to see that he's not a teacher anymore; he's now the person who is responsible for the quality of the teachers' work."

As an alternative example, a leadership coach working with an administrator who did understand how to identify effective instruction helped the administrator by honing her skills to offer constructive feedback to teachers. The leadership coach conducted a formal classroom observation of a teacher with the principal and then commented on the principal's "write-up" of the observation. The coach made suggestions for the new administrator that illustrated how the principal might suggest ways for the teacher to improve her instruction as well as to point to specific practices that appeared to be lacking in the classroom—or that were lacking during the observation.

In both cases, the coach combined the evidence they gathered, the questions they raised, and the reflection prompted during coaching sessions to help the new principals see what it was that was missing. Whether done through modeling or by critiquing a new principal's work, the coaches effectively engaged three aspects of the purposeful coaching model in order to help the principals develop an instructional routine that, as one coach noted, "would lead to better instruction ... which is the ultimate goal of coaching, really."

MONITORING THE NEW PRINCIPAL'S ACTIONS

As a final point, the coaches each monitored the new principal's actions throughout the coaching process. They did so by continuing to ask questions and gather evidence and, at times, by holding the principals accountable for actions that they pledged to take in previous coaching sessions. As one leadership coach noted, "You're always trying to help the principal find an entry point ... the point where they can begin to exercise some leadership." The leadership coaches indicated that clarifying and prioritizing issues often preceded other efforts to help the principals address the issues in their buildings.

In one example, an elementary school principal reported that her leadership coach helped her understand how one of her decisions had adversely impacted the school and her relationship with teachers.

According to the principal, she surveyed classroom teachers at the beginning of the school year to determine how satisfied teachers were with the school as well as what the teachers were interested in doing. One teacher indicated that he would like to move from the classroom and take over the school's physical education program if the teacher who was currently in that position retired. When the existing teacher announced his retirement, the principal posted the position and hired a candidate from outside the building. In response, the fourth-grade teacher who wanted the position applied for another position in a different school and announced that he would be leaving. When informed of the teacher's decision, the principal was surprised.

In this situation, the coach helped the principal unpack the situation, seeing why the teacher was upset and helping the principal connect the outcome (the teacher leaving) with her decision to post the position. According to the leadership coach,

> What the principal did not understand was that her decision to post and hire from the outside isolated the fourth-grade teacher.... It was like she passed judgment on his ability to teach PE, when it was clear to everyone in the building that he wanted to teach PE.... A more experienced principal might have realized that in this situation one of the first things she should have done was to approach the teacher and determine whether (a) they were still interested and (b) if they were interested, whether they were the best candidate for the position. Since she didn't do this, she upset the teacher and basically he responded by leaving—even though she admitted that he was a very good teacher.

Based on the situation, the coach indicated she felt "a more experienced principal would have understood the importance of maintaining that relationship ... especially if they valued that teacher and the skills that they brought to the building." When interviewed, the principal indicated that she had likely mismanaged the situation. "I think had I known what the outcome would be, or thought ahead to that point, I would have been more cautious about making the decisions that I did.... I could have prevented what ultimately happened."

In this case, the coach noted the actions taken by the principal as well as the outcome that resulted from the principal's actions. When the new principal approached a similar staffing issue, the coach raised the point with the new principal. As the coach explained, "I sort of put that issue in the bank and when it was time I pulled it out again.... I tried to do it before she made a similar decision as a way to learn from the past." When the coach raised the issue the new principal reported that she saw what the coach was trying to do and recognized what she needed to do differently in light of her past experience. "I think the whole thing went more smoothly because I was reminded what happened before.... I saw that I needed to ask the teachers who might want the position first before I posted it."

ACCELERATING PRINCIPAL DEVELOPMENT THROUGH LEADERSHIP COACHING

The results of this study suggest that leadership coaching may accelerate principal development as instructional leaders and elements of the purposeful coaching model may contribute to this development. The model's emphasis on helping principals clarify and prioritize issues in their schools, develop an instructional routine, and maintain relationships with classroom teachers appeared instrumental in providing the new principals with the skills they needed to influence the instruction in their schools. These findings are consistent with existing research, which has identified strong connections between a principal's instructional leadership practice and school-level instructional capacity that contributes to student learning (Heck & Hallinger, 2009; Robinson, Lloyd, & Rowe, 2008). Coaches helped principals identify issues that they could address through their leadership practice. This was found to be important in recent research on principal leadership (Portin et al., 2009). Although the issues presented here are primarily related to teaching and learning, data from this study implies that coaches may provide equally helpful support to new principals on operational issues as well.

While additional research is needed on the specific ways that coaches support principals, and the impact that leadership coaching has on principal leadership practice, the results obtained in this study suggest that leadership coaches were instrumental in at least one area—helping them maintain a focus on classroom instruction through the development of an instructional routine. As Stein and Nelson (2003) suggested in their discussion of leadership content knowledge, understanding what good instruction looks like and how to improve instruction overall is an essential skill that all principals should possess.

The findings from this research also have important implications for the preparation of education leaders. The study reveals that university-based leadership coaching is a powerful form of induction for new school leaders and that it may be a natural extension to traditional preparation experiences. While university-based leadership coaching has not developed as fully as other induction programs, the results of this study indicate that universities may have a viable, indeed powerful, role in providing induction support for new principals. In doing so, university-based programs may fill an important void in the support provided to new principals. This model of leadership coaching could also apply to central office administrators and teacher leaders. For example, the Purposeful Coaching Model articulated by the program could potentially assist central office administrators who serve as principal supervisors in identifying challenges that their principals are facing and determining how they can best support principals in responding to those challenges. Similarly, principals might utilize the PCM in their work with teacher leaders to clarify and prioritize instructional challenges that these teacher leaders might address with their colleagues in classrooms.

Beyond the implications that the model has for practice, we also find that the findings from this study have implications for the preparation of school principals. In each of the cases we described, the principals completed a university-based preparation program with a traditional curriculum focused on the principal as an instructional leader. However, once in the field, the findings from this study suggest that the principals lacked an understanding of instructional leadership in actual practice, and that the coaches ultimately were helpful in providing the new principals with support that led to their understanding of and comfort in using instructional leadership strategies in their schools.

Related to this, the PCM may have implications for the preparation of leadership coaches. Our findings indicate that effective preparation of leadership coaches focuses on core "moves" or "strategies" that enable the coach to identify principals' needs and develop a response to them. We find that the type of questions the coaches employ, the nature of evidence that coaches collect, and the extent to which the coaches engage the new principals in reflection are especially important in determining how fully the coaching support impacts principals' practice. Further research about how coaches enact the PCM is needed to determine when and how coaches employ different elements of the model and the conditions that prompt them to do so. The findings of this research will likely have implications for the development of the coaching model and further refinement of training opportunities for coaches.

REFERENCES

Anderson, M. E. (1991). *Principals: How to train, recruit, select, induct, and evaluate leaders for America's schools*. Eugene, OR: ERIC Clearinghouse on Educational Management.

Barnett, B. G. (1995). Developing reflection and expertise: Can mentors make the difference? *Journal of Educational Administration, 3*(5), 45–59.

Bloom, G., Castagna, C., Moir, E., & Warren, B. (2005). *Blended coaching: Skills and strategies to support principal development*. Thousand Oaks, CA: Corwin Press.

Creswell, J. W. (1998). *Qualitative inquiry and research design: Choosing among five traditions*. Thousand Oaks, CA: SAGE.

Crow, G. M., & Matthews, L. J. (1998). *Finding one's way: How mentoring can lead to dynamic leadership*. Thousand Oaks, CA: Corwin Press.

Daresh, J. C. (2004). Mentoring school leaders: Professional promise or predictable problems? *Educational Administration Quarterly, 40*(4), 495–517

Gates, S. M., Ringel, J. S., Santibañez, L., Guarino, C., Ghosh-Dastidar, B., & Brown, A. (2006). Mobility and turnover among school principals. *Economics of Education Review, 25*(3), 289–02.

Hall, P. (2008). Building bridges: Strengthening the principal induction process through intentional mentoring. *Phi Delta Kappan, 89*(6), 449–452.

Hargrove, R. (1995). *Masterful coaching: Extraordinary results by impacting people and the way they think and work together.* San Francisco: Jossey-Bass.

Hart, A. W. (1993). *Principal succession: Establishing leadership in schools.* Albany: State University of New York Press.

Heck, R. H., & Hallinger, P. (2009). Assessing the contribution of distributed leadership to school improvement and growth in math achievement. *American Educational Research Journal. 46*(3), 659–689.

Lortie, D. C. (2009). *School principal: Managing in public.* Chicago: University of Chicago Press.

Malone, R. J. (2001, Winter). Principal mentoring. *Research Roundup: National Association of Elementary School Principals*, p. 1.

Merriam, S. B. (1998). *Qualitative research and case study applications in education.* San Francisco: Jossey-Bass.

Miles, M. B., & Huberman, A. M. (1994). *Qualitative data analysis* (2nd ed.). Thousand Oaks, CA: SAGE.

Papa, F., Jr., & Baxter, I. A. (2005). Dispelling the myths and confirming the truths of the imminent shortage of principals: The case of New York State. *Planning and Changing, 36*(3/4), 217–234.

Parkay, F. W., Currie, G., & Rhodes, J. W. (1992). Professional socialization: A longitudinal study of twelve high school principals. *Educational Administration Quarterly, 28*, 43–75.

Patton, M. Q. (2002). *Qualitative research and evaluation methods* (3rd ed.). Thousand Oaks, CA: SAGE.

Portin, B. S., Knapp, M. S., Dareff, S., Feldman, S., Russell, F. A., Samuelson, C., et al. (2009). *Leadership for learning improvement in urban schools.* Seattle: Center for the Study of Teaching and Policy, University of Washington.

Pounder, D. G., Galvin, P., & Shepherd, P. (2003). An analysis of the United States educational administrator shortage. *Australian Journal of Education, 47*(2), 133–145.

Reeves, J., Moos, L., & Forrest, J. (1998). The school leader's view. In J. Macbeth (Ed.), *Effective school leadership* (pp. 32–59). London: Paul Chapman/SAGE.

Reiss, K. (2007). *Leadership coaching for educators: Bringing out the best in school administrators.* Thousand Oaks, CA: Corwin Press.

Ribbins, P. (1998, June). *On ladders and greasy poles: Developing school leaders' careers.* Paper presented at the Third ESRC Seminar, Milton Keynes, UK.

Robinson, V. M. J., Lloyd, C. A., & Rowe, K. J. (2008). The impact of leadership on student outcomes: An analysis of the differential effects of leadership types. *Educational Administration Quarterly, 44* (5), 635–673.

Rowan, B. (1995). Learning, teaching, and educational administration: Toward a research agenda. *Educational Administration Quarterly, 31*(3), 344–354.

Roza, M., Celio, M. B., Harvey, J., & Wilson, S. (2003, January). *A matter of definition: Is there truly a shortage of school principals?* Seattle, WA: Center on Reinventing Public Education.

Schainker, S. A., & Roberts, L. M. (1987). Helping principals overcome on-the-job obstacles. *Educational Leadership, 45*(1), 30–33.

Spillane, J. P., Halverson, R., & Diamond, J. B. (2001). Investigating school leadership practice: A distributed perspective. *Educational Researcher, 30*(3), 23–28.

Spillane, J. P., Hallett, T., & Diamond, J. B. (2003). Forms of capital and the construction of leadership: Instructional leadership in urban elementary schools. *Sociology of Education, 76*(1), 1–17.

Spiro, J., Mattis, M. C., & Mitgang, L. D. (2007). *Getting principal mentoring right: Lessons from the field.* New York: The Wallace Foundation.

Stein, M. K., & Nelson, B. S. (2003). Leadership content knowledge. *Educational Evaluation and Policy Analysis, 25*(4), 423–448.

Stringer, E. T. (2003). *Action research in education.* Upper Saddle River, NJ: Prentice Hall.

Strober, D. R., & Grant, A. M. (2006). Toward a contextual approach to coaching models. In D.R. Strober & A. M. Grant (Eds.), *Evidence-based coaching handbook: Putting best practices to work for your clients* (pp. 355–366). Hoboken, NJ: Wiley.

Villani, S. (2006). *Mentoring and induction programs that support new principals.* Thousand Oaks, CA: Corwin Press.

Weindling, D. (2000, April). *Stages of headship: A longitudinal study of the principalship.* Paper presented at the annual meeting of the American Educational Research Association, New Orleans, LA.

Whitaker, K. S. (2002). Principal role changes and influence on principal recruitment and selection. *Journal of Education Administration, 41*(1), 37–54

Wilmore, E. W. (2004). *Principal induction: A standards-based model for administrator development.* Thousand Oaks, CA: Corwin Press.

Winter, R., Burroughs, S., & Burroughs, S. (1989). *Learning from experience: Principles and practice in action research.* London: Falmer Press.

CHAPTER 6

FROM MENTORING
TO COACHING

Finding the Path to
Support for Beginning Principals

John C. Daresh

The use of successful, experienced school principals to serve as mentors for newly-appointed principals has long been a widely used practice in the United States and in many other nations (Crow & Matthews, 1998; Hobson, 2003; Holcomb, 1989; Riggins-Newby & Zarlengo, 2003; Walker & Stott, 1993; Weingartner, 2009). Over the past 25 years, providing support for beginning school principals through the involvement of mentors has become a mandated activity (albeit, rarely supported financially) in many states, including Ohio, Colorado, Illinois, and others (Daresh, 2004). However, initial mandates have not always served to ensure the continuation of mentoring. Programs have been costly (salaries or stipends have been needed to reward principal mentors), and highly labor-intensive (those serving as mentors have frequently been expected to provide support for novice leaders while continuing to carry out other duties). As a result, principal mentoring has often been seen as a practice

The Challenges for New Principals in the Twenty-First Century:
Developing Leadership Capabilities Through Professional Support, pp. 121–145
Copyright © 2010 by Information Age Publishing
All rights of reproduction in any form reserved.

whose time has come, but that time has often appeared to be a time that left as quickly as it came (Daresh, 2004).

The assumption underlying mentoring for new principals rests on the belief that when an individual first assumes the role of school leader, he or she should be matched with a colleague who can provide ongoing information to a newcomer so that the novice could face the realities of a new job with a degree of confidence and a personal sense of competence (Daresh & Playko, 1991, 1992; Tooms, 2003). Typically, information provided by the mentor is assumed to deal with procedural or technical matters such as budgeting, scheduling, parent involvement, and many similar administrative duties with which a beginning principal might feel insecure during the first years of service. A traditional belief has been that an experienced administrator would have the knowledge needed to offer a new colleague advice that would enable a smooth transition into a new professional role (Bolam, McMahon, Pocklington, & Weindling, 1995). Without a doubt, this approach to mentoring is meant to be insurance to guard against an unsuccessful start to a new professional role (Lindley, 2005). In the program described in this chapter, this objective of mentoring was only part of the intention of designers. The ELIS Project of the Chicago Public Schools is an effort to increase the likelihood that newly-appointed principals will serve as instructional leaders, not simply "survive the first year."

CHICAGO PUBLIC SCHOOLS AND THE ELIS PROJECT

The Chicago Public Schools (CPS) is a huge urban school district. With nearly one-half million students in 700 school buildings, it ranks as the third largest school district in the United States. During the past 20 years, the district has undergone significant changes in its efforts to respond to many of the issues that have served as challenges in most school districts across the nation. Among these have been how to: (1) improve learning and achievement by students (Sebring & Bryk, 2000) regardless of socio-economic, racial, linguistic, or ethnic backgrounds; (2) increase parental and community involvement in schools; and (3) reduce violence, truancy, dropout rates, and other indicators of schools that have lost touch with a sense of the need for public schools to provide adequate, safe, and secure educational experiences.

Another challenge facing U.S. schools is related to the importance of developing ways in which educational leaders can be better supported in their efforts to direct more effective instructional programs in schools. It has been more than 3 decades since the work by Edmonds (1981), Austin

(1979), and many others showing the relationship between instruction-focused leadership by school principals and discernible improvement in educational achievement. As Lipham (1981) noted, "Effective principals, effective schools."

While the importance of principals serving as leaders of learning has been well documented (Heck & Hallinger, 2009) and accepted as a goal to improve educational practice, the role of the principal has become increasingly demanding. Besides focusing on instruction, they are responsible for ensuring their schools are safe and secure learning environments while working effectively with parents and other community groups in sharing decision making related to school improvement. Most recently, demands for greater accountability for increased levels of student achievement have become the focus of all principals (McGhee & Nelson, 2005; Portin & Shen, 1998). In short, the world has gone beyond the conventional image of the school principal as a building manager. Instructional leadership now has a much more precise definition than it might have had in the early 1980s. In their analysis of the type of leadership behaviors that seem to bring about improvements in student learning, Fink and Resnick (2001) noted that instructional leadership is an approach to leading a school where a principal creates "a culture of learning" created by "the right kinds of specialized professional development opportunities" (p. 599). Instructional leaders demonstrate skills in fostering the best practices by classroom teachers who deliver instruction to students each day.

At least in part because of the increasing pressures now placed on principals, their job has become decreasingly popular as a career target for many educators. Of course, many other factors have led to this decline of interest. Salaries of administrators are no longer sufficiently better than those of classroom teachers in many school districts to warrant moving into jobs with greater stress, pressure, longer hours, and higher degrees of conflict. School districts across the country are experiencing increases in student enrollment while opportunities for early retirement mean that many school systems struggle to find individuals willing to take on the challenges of the principalship (Fink & Resnick, 2001).

Large and small districts face these issues; however, in the "mega-districts" of the United States, each serving more than a quarter of a million students, the need for new people to assume principalships is reaching a crisis point. Districts like Chicago, New York, Los Angeles, Miami/Dade County, Philadelphia, and Houston must hire dozens if not hundreds of new principals each year. More importantly, the people expected to fill openings in large urban systems must be extremely capable and dedicated to making a difference in the learning and achievement of students.

The Effective Leaders Improve Schools (ELIS) Project in Chicago was launched with resources provided by the U.S. Department of Education, the City of Chicago, and the Wallace Foundation. ELIS began with the 2005–06 school year. The grant and activities related to the professional development of principals in the Chicago Public Schools (CPS) was assigned to the Office of Principal Preparation and Development (OPPD), a unit created in 2003 to ensure that each school would be led by an effective principal by enhancing the quality of the pool of principal candidates, supporting the selection of outstanding principals for every school, and supporting principal success. There are many dimensions of ELIS, but this chapter is limited to a review of one important activity, namely mentoring and coaching for beginning CPS principals.

Dimensions of ELIS

The project was initially funded because of its potential to achieve three goals:

1. Mentors provide direct and purposeful support to help aspiring or new principals to perform at a high level and make observable progress toward becoming transformational instructional leaders.
2. Mentors and mentees connect leadership development efforts to improvement needs in the school, resulting in positive impact on the quality of teaching and learning as evidenced by measurable gains in student achievement.
3. The mentoring relationship is an integrated component of meeting the professional needs of the mentee, as the mentor uses blended coaching strategies to improve targeted, appropriate, and timely learning and development opportunities to aspiring and new school leaders.

An important event assisting in the development of more effective leaders came about prior to the initiation of ELIS through a year-long process involving a Blue Ribbon Committee comprised of educational and community leaders who came together to identify the critical skills that need to be mastered by effective CPS principals (Cunat & Daresh, 2007). The result was the creation of five CPS Principal Competencies, which state that effective Chicago principals:

1. *Develop and articulate a belief system through voice and action* (e.g., leading by example, involving all members of the school

community in providing support for instruction and striving to achieve a common vision).

2. *Engage and develop faculty* (e.g., developing leadership among teachers, supporting staff development, aligning staff development with school goals, and recruiting and retaining quality teachers).

3. *Assess the quality of classroom instruction* (e.g., using knowledge of learning theories and practices, leading standards-based instruction, and using data to improve instruction and student achievement).

4. *Facilitate and motivate change* (e.g., understanding the change process for individuals and organizations, being committed to children and having high expectations for learning, and facilitating shared responsibility regarding change efforts).

5. *Balance management* (e.g., delegating effectively when needed, aligning resources to instructional needs).

During the first 2 years of ELIS, individuals were designated as mentors to more than 200 first-year CPS principals. In the third year of the program, the use of the term "mentors" ceased, and "leadership coaches" were employed to work with less-experienced colleagues. The use of "coaches" was the result of the annual data collection process described in this chapter. There was also a conscious effort to separate ELIS strategies from previous norms and practices. For instance, "mentoring" for new principals was widely used for the past 20 years to signify "torch passing," but this process was losing its relevance since the duties of CPS principals have been changing so rapidly in recent years. ELIS is dedicated to two broad foci: (1) to enable beginning Chicago principals to "hit the ground running" to become leaders for learning and (2) to support urban principals beyond being building managers. Although research conducted with newly-appointed headteachers in the United Kingdom suggested that novices have management concerns that they want advice from mentors, they also noted that carrying out assigned managerial tasks was not sufficient for success in leading a school (Pocklington & Weindling, 1996). Chicago's schools will depend increasingly on the ability of principals to serve as instructional leaders. That is the central task of all who served as coaches or mentors.

This chapter examines how effectively mentors and coaches were able to guide new principals faced with managing their schools while also ensuring effective teaching and learning. The discussion focuses on the central question: In what ways can mentors and coaches go beyond supporting beginning as competent managers so they become principals who "make a difference" in student learning?

Mentoring Arrangements: Year I

ELIS grant resources were utilized to enhance the quality of two mentoring programs for principals and future principals that already existed in CPS. Previously, the Chicago Principals and Administrators Association (CPAA) and the Chicago Academy for School Leadership (CASL) (Anderson, 2001) offered programs that made use of experienced principals as mentors. One was LAUNCH, which existed to support the efforts of aspiring principals who worked with experienced principals to learn about the skills needed to manage efficient schools. Mentors also worked with another program, LIFT, to help beginning principals learn critical management skills. While both programs were viewed positively, they were limited to assisting individuals in acquiring technical skills, rather than the instructional leadership goals, objectives, and vision found in the CPS Principal Competencies. The expectation was that ELIS would enable the district to move mentoring to a new level of professional development for beginning principals. During the first year of ELIS (2005–06), beginning principal mentor activity was documented through a Quality Assurance process (Cunat & Daresh, 2007) to monitor the effectiveness of interactions between novices and mentors.

Ongoing review was clearly specified as essential to determine what, if any, impact mentoring of new principals related to increased student learning. Quality Assurance was designed to:

1. Determine the apparent impact of mentoring activity on new principals' abilities to grow professionally in the five CPS Principal Competencies.
2. Ascertain the impact of mentoring on new principals' capacity to address the improvement needs in their schools.
3. Ensure the quality of mentoring interactions taking place to promote new principals' reflections about improving overall professional practice.

The Principal Mentoring Quality Assurance Reflection Instrument (Appendix A) was administered to mentors and novice principals twice during the 2005–06 school year. The instrument was to be completed by mentors and mentees who would also collaborate in preparing the Principal Mentoring Quality Assurance Report. This was to allow mentors and new principals to reflect on the types of activities that were working in their relationships, areas in need of improvement, strategies for improvement, and additional support needed from the district. This instrument was to be returned to the OPPD in December 2005 and March 2006.

A second instrument, the Induction Mentor Support Log, was completed by mentors each month, prior to the receipt of stipend payments. This document required the designation of the amount of time spent in face-to-face support from mentors to mentees, as well as other mentor/new principal interactions and contacts that occurred.

A third instrument was offered as a resource to promote dialogue concerning the content of interactions. The tool was designed to assist mentors and mentees to co-create subsequent agendas for their work together. This instrument, a Collaborative Log, was adapted from the blended coaching work of Bloom, Castagna, Moir, and Warren (2005).

Results of the Year One Quality Assurance. After the first year of ELIS, OPPD staff reviewed input from mentors and mentees, noting limitations of the quality of the data received. On one hand, participants expressed satisfaction with mentoring, indicating they appreciated the investments in their professional development. Mentors also mentioned that they had the opportunity to contribute to colleagues' growth. On the other hand, several questions arose from the CPS data after 1 year: (1) Were mentors and novices engaged in conversations related to professional development framed by the Competencies? (2) Was there evidence that mentees acted differently during their first year as school principals? and (3) Were mentors witnessing development or simply the enjoyment of listening to frustrations and concerns of new principals on a regular basis? Although there were positive outcomes expressed by novices and mentors, they tended to provide general statements of satisfaction as illustrated by these comments: "I have a clear understanding of the goals and objectives of mentoring." "What I share with my mentee will be critical to her success as an urban principal." "Our mentoring interactions help establish the mentee as an instructional leader from the onset of the new principalship." The few negative remarks dealt with logistical concerns, such as having enough time to work with mentees, ability to meet as often as desired with mentees, and having enough time to negotiate the mentoring relationship.

Therefore, as the first-year data were analyzed, OPPD staff raised questions that needed to be considered in the future:

1. Are new principals learning how to implement the CPS Principal Competencies as part of their behavior as leaders?
2. Are new principals approaching their work more thoughtfully because of their interactions with mentors?
3. Are new principals' preconceived notions about the principalship being confirmed or challenged?

4. Are new principals demonstrating behaviors more consistent with instructional leaders, as contrasted with building managers? If so, what interventions by mentors appeared to be effective in bringing about such behaviors?

Mentoring Arrangements: Year II

Based on the analysis of the quality assurance instrument process, changes were made to the data collection involving 65 mentors and 124 new principals participating in Year II of ELIS (2006–07). First, the term "quality assurance" was replaced by "mentoring impact" to more accurately reflect the goal of data collection. The questionnaire title was changed to Mentoring Impact Instrument (see Appendix B). Some Year 1 participants found the term "quality assurance" offensive because it suggested that data collected were meant primarily to ensure that mentors were "doing what they were paid to do." The view by many was that OPPD staff members were using data only to "check up on" mentors. Second, information was collected using Mentoring Impact Instruments on three occasions during the school year (November, February, and June). In Year I, mentors and mentees admitted that they rarely used their limited time together to complete the Quality Assurance Instruments. Many admitted that they simply completed the instruments just before they were due to OPPD.

Finally, using the data collection intentionally sought information about the use of CPS Principal Competencies. The first Competencies to be addressed were numbers 1 ("Articulating a Belief System through Voice and Action") and 5 ("Balance Management"). These items reflected issues that were most likely of immediate concern to newly-appointed principals during the first few weeks of their jobs. Research on leadership succession has often shown that the ability to appreciate personal values is a critical skill for any beginning leader (Daresh, 1986; Hart, 1993; Weindling & Earley, 1987). Beginners are also overwhelmed with efforts to understand the need to balance leadership expectations with management duties. The second and third administrations of the Mentoring Impact Instruments addressed the other three Competencies ("Engaging and Developing Faculty," "Assessing the Quality of Classroom Instruction," and "Facilitating and Motivating Change").

Results of Year II Mentoring Impact. Efforts to ensure a better match between the goals of ELIS and actual practices carried out by mentors and first-year principals resulted in substantial modifications in data collection. In Year II, there were two different forms of the Mentoring Impact Instrument created, one for mentors and one for mentees. Respondents were asked to be more precise about the ways in which mentoring brought about change in the behavior of new principals during their first year on the job. The following are examples of the impact of the mentoring process, from the perspective of mentees:

> [Regarding the articulation of belief systems,] my mentor is well versed in the school's culture and the dynamics of stakeholders. As a result, our discussions and analyses bend me toward gaining significant insights regarding the school's existing beliefs and how to effectively engage all stakeholders.

> [When articulating a belief system,] my mentor is aware of the absolute necessity for the school leader to be capable of defining and sharing his or her vision with all stakeholders. My thinking has been impacted by this professional relationship because my mentor is not trying to shape my principalship. Instead, he had promoted a relationship from which we can learn from one another."

> [In terms of balanced management,] he has been genuine in sharing his outlook on balancing management. He has expressed a belief that balancing management will continue to evolve as different challenges present themselves and to trust your instinct as a leader when it comes to trade-offs that will inevitably have to be made within the management framework. This insight has been encouraging my own thinking about balancing management and has kept this competency vivid in my own mind in our regular communications.

The Competencies dealing with skills traditionally associated with instructional leadership (Reitzug & West, 2009) focus on developing faculty (Competency #2) and assessing classroom instruction (Competency #3). Responses of new principals and mentors supported the emergence of new principals' abilities in these critical areas:

> My mentor has significantly influenced my thinking about assessing the quality of instruction. I am vigilant and committed to quality instruction, and I continuously engage in reflective thought regarding key elements that lead to the delivery and assessment of quality instruction.

> We [mentor and new principal] have reviewed professional literature and research on practices that have been shown to improve the achievement of low-income, inner-city students and reflected on implementation of practices in my school.

> My mentor is committed to quality instruction. She has worked with me to analyze data to use it in planning for quality instruction that meets the needs of students by considering strengths, weaknesses, and needs of an increasing bilingual population were recognized by using this data, especially vocabulary development and math problems. Teachers are expanding their instruction to address these considerations.

During Year II, it was clear that the Competencies framework was an effective device to ensure that mentor-mentee conversations were more clearly linked to revealing how mentoring was affecting the thinking and behaviors of novice principals. Mentors were beginning to engage in more intentional discussions related to ways in which novice principals could become engaged in activity related to faculty development and instructional improvement.

Mentoring Arrangements: Year III

Providing assistance to a large number of inexperienced CPS principals continued into a third year during 2007–08. The net result of fine-tuning the mentoring process during the first 2 years yielded a more useful and accurate way of assessing the impact of structured mentoring for newcomers. Year III of ELIS required additional refinements because 170 new principals were hired in 2007. The large number of novice principals required changing the ways in which support could be provided to them (Daresh, Best, Shay, & Alexander, 2008). Finding and preparing enough effective mentors demanded that current principals would no longer be asked to serve as mentors. Only recent principal retirees (within the past 5 years) from the Chicago Public Schools would be considered as mentor candidates to work with up to seven new principals. Furthermore, the word "mentor" was changed to "coach," signifying a stand-alone post for retired principals who could devote full-time assistance for the professional development of novices. The term "coach" also implied a job description that would include one-on-one as well as small-group work with first-year principals. When coaches had completed their work with their set of first-year principals, they would be considered candidates to continue working with principals in their second year. The change of job title represented a school system making assistance to principals by other principals a new and important professional role to promote school improvement. Other changes initiated in the third year are described below.

Rigorous Recruitment and Selection of Coaches. In Year III, clear qualifications were specified for leadership coach applicants. First, coaches were drawn only from the ranks of recently-retired CPS principals. Second, applicants had to provide evidence that they were effective in leading high-quality instructional programs, where student achievement had shown improvement over the three most recent years of their service. No longer would references from people with political "clout" suffice as sole evidence of effectiveness. In addition, they were asked to provide written statements concerning their views on the needs of beginning principals and how coaching would be a useful practice for novice administrators. Finally, each candidate participated in an interview with OPPD staff. Twenty individuals were named leadership coaches for the 170 new principals during the 2007–08 school year.

Summer Leadership Coach Training Seminar. Coaches were required to attend training designed to enable them to appreciate the importance of relationship development by using the phases of coaching proposed by Zachary (2005), and understand the need to contribute to a coaching community of practice. Coaches were also provided with an orientation to ELIS, the importance of the CPS Principal Competencies, and expectations associated with service as leadership coaches. Coaches also met and began planning with their protégées ("coachees") before the school year began.

Blended Coaching Training. All CPS Leadership Coaches participated in training related to blended coaching (Bloom et al., 2005). This model is based on the assumption that effective coaching is built on relationship building, listening, observing, questioning, and giving feedback—behaviors described as activities of principals identified as "instructional leaders" (Hoerr, 1996; Mackey, Pitcher, & Decman, 2006; Robinson & Temperley, 2007). Blended coaching promotes transforming traditional mentoring from an activity where mentors "tell" mentees what to do; instead, it is an activity based on promoting personal development that drives the learning process.

The training sessions enabled coaches to learn the differences that exist among instructional, facilitative, and collaborative, or transformational coaching. These approaches may be used at different times to provide appropriate support. Too often, mentoring and coaching programs rely on experienced principals using only instructional methodologies (i.e., they "tell" mentees or coaches what they are "supposed to do at all times").

The annual reviews of the first 2 years of ELIS indicated that there may have been appreciation for mentoring, but there was discontent that mentors often simply told novices how to behave. There was little effort to guide beginning principals through a reflective process where they could discover appropriate solutions to problems on their own. In many cases, novice principals were given only one way to address issues in their schools. Since ELIS sought to ensure that a change in the ways in which principals led their schools would take place, induction supporting new ways of looking at some problems was needed. Blended coaching offered a chance to break away from the traditions of what had been an apprenticeship model for new principals.

Leadership Coach Networking and Support Sessions. Year III featured monthly meetings of all leadership coaches. These meetings included opportunities for the assembled group to share concerns about the work that was taking place with new principals in the field and practice blended coaching strategies. These sessions also enabled units from within CPS to share updated information about policies and practices with the coaches who could pass along information about district developments to novice principals.

Rapid Response Team. In the first 2 years of ELIS, most contacts between mentors and beginning principals involved discussions of management issues. That was not surprising; however, expecting mentors to spend most of their time working with new principals to improve instructional leadership skills was not a realistic goal since beginning principals often feel as if they are constantly under pressure to manage their schools. Feedback from mentors and new principals during the first 2 years of ELIS noted an inordinate amount of time being used to address managerial concerns. Therefore, current and retired principals who were not coaches became members of the Rapid Response Team (RRT). The purpose of the RRT was to provide novices with expertise in specific management areas, such as budgeting, contract management, and scheduling, which tended to be short-term issues, not long-term leadership development leading to more effective instruction and student learning. The creation of the RRT was to enable coaches to engage with new principals in ways that differ from traditional discussions of "beans, busses, and budgets."

Results of Year III Coaching Impact. The Coaching Impact Instrument asked coaches and new principals to provide insights on three occasions during the third year of ELIS similar to the same issues examined in Year II. While the questions asked remained virtually the same in the third year, some important changes were made in the coaching process. Full-time coaches were now used and they were selected more carefully, intensive training was required of all coaches, many coaches met with their group of new principals several times during the year, monthly meetings of coaches were held, and efforts were made to decrease the tendency for coaches to spend most of their time "fixing" immediate managerial concerns. The question asked was whether coaching appeared to be making a difference in terms of assisting new principals to become instructional leaders. One additional practice emerged in Year III and it appeared to have a positive impact on the overall program. In the third year, consultants reviewed the findings from the Coaching Impact Instruments with coaches, pointing out issues and trends found in the data reviewed (Barnett & Daresh, 2007).

As coaching impact data were analyzed throughout Year III, the following observations were made:

- First-year principals expressed appreciation for the project, as it served to support people in their first years.

- Responses provided by coaches and coachees in Year III indicated that there was focused effort on the Competencies throughout the year. Also, because coaches were no longer required to address as many managerial issues as they had in the past, they were more likely to "stay on script" and work on different Principal Competencies throughout the year.

- There was evidence of the value of blended coaching training on the behavior of the coaches throughout Year III. In the first administration of the instrument in November, the coaches and new principals engaged in discussions in which directive or instructional coaching was being used. This seemed appropriate for cases where the two parties were coming together for the first time. Trust was not yet established to the point where more open two-way learning could occur.

- In the second and third administrations of the instrument (February and June), instructional coaching continued, but not as the predominant strategy used by coaches working with new principals. Conscious efforts were being made by coaches to incorporate indirect coaching approaches as the year progressed. By the third administration of the Coaching Impact Instrument, it was clear that coaching conferences were increasingly being led by beginning principals; coaches were no longer setting or controlling the agendas.

- Topics of discussion between coaches and new principals were increasingly focused on instructional, rather than managerial, issues.

WHAT WAS LEARNED FROM ELIS?

Reviewing the ELIS mentoring program yielded insights not only about practices associated with this program, but also about efforts to provide mentoring support for beginning school principals in general. Overall, the following conclusions can be drawn:

1. Determine specific ways mentoring activities are helping new principals to think about and use desired competencies.

2. Ascertain the impact of mentoring on new principals' capacities to address the improvement needs of their schools.

3. Attend to the quality of mentoring interactions taking place to promote new principals' reflections about improving their professional practice.

Each of these conclusions is elaborated below.

Value of Competencies to Guide Mentoring. There appeared to be subtle but real progress over the 3 years of the ELIS Project regarding the reliance on the Competencies as guides for mentors and new school leaders. Year I saw few references made to the Competencies. Two factors may explain this observation. First, the data collection instruments did not directly seek information from either mentors or new principals in terms of progress being made in the areas of developing and articulating a belief system, engaging and developing faculty, assessing the quality of classroom instruction, facilitating and motivating change, or balancing management with leadership demands. While the Competencies were developed through a process that involved many different stakeholders across Chicago, they were still somewhat novel to many new and experienced principals. Principals had been selected largely through traditional patterns of seeking jobs in the city, and that was through the presentation of prior administrative experience to local school councils (LSC) who actually hired the principals. In many instances, those who could convince LSC members that they had sufficient prior experience in CPS to be able to "do the job" were chosen as administrators. Just before the launch of the ELIS Project, that process was altered by OPPD, requiring all applicants for principalships to prepare portfolios showing their level of skills regarding the five Competencies. This competency-based "eligibility process" was used with few of the 90 newly appointed principals for CPS in the 2005–06 school year. Therefore, many novice principals only knew about the Competencies; they had not been affected by the emerging vision of what it meant to be an effective Chicago principal.

The second factor affecting the lack of attention devoted the Competencies in Year I was that mentors were simply not aware of the expectations for these statements. While they knew about the Competencies, mentors perceived their roles largely in terms of providing management advice to beginners. Often, mentor-mentee dialogue consisted of mentors sharing recollections of how they addressed administrative problems in their own careers, without any reference to the Competencies.

However, Years II and III were marked by increased focus on the Competencies during mentor–mentee discussions. Some of this may have been because a higher percentage of the 124 new principals in 2006–07 had become familiar with the CPS Competencies as part of the new eligibility process, connecting the Competency statements to their experiences as teacher leaders. In addition, after Year I, the decision was made to reduce the number of mentors; some mentors were not invited to continue with the project largely because they continued to view their roles as passive consultants who offered advice only when it was sought by beginning principals. Subsequently, mentors selected to participate were provided with more specific training related to the use of the Competencies to guide their interactions with mentees. Finally, instruments designed to gain information about the impact of mentoring in Years II and III were designed specifically to determine how the Competencies were being addressed in mentoring or coaching interactions. Also, implementing the Rapid Response Team in Year III freed up a great deal of time for coaches to engage in more deliberate conversations with their coachees concerning progress in each of the Competencies.

Mentoring Impact on School Improvement. Chicago Public Schools (and all of the public schools in the state of Illinois) are required to engage in an annual school improvement planning process that involves a review of the past year's performance and achievement by students, improvement goals for the following school year, and strategies to be followed to achieve intended improvement goals. In Chicago, this activity is referred to as SIPAA (School Improvement Planning for Academic Achievement) planning. Interactions between mentors/coaches and new principals in this area consisted of three stages carried out throughout each school year. Early in their interactions, mentors and novices had conversations regarding the nature of the SIPAA that principals inherited from their predecessors. In most cases, beginning principals had no prior knowledge about their schools, other than the raw data they received regarding the past school year's student achievement performance. Beginning principals then worked with their experienced colleagues in reviewing data without the benefit of two critical pieces of information: (1) the culture of their new schools in terms of teacher-student interaction, parental involvement and expectations, and student attitudes toward school and (2) the feasibility of using the stated follow-up goals and strategies planned for achieving their SIPAA goals.

Therefore, the experience of mentors was valued by newcomers in considering approaches that new principals might use in ascertaining whether goals and strategies in their new schools were likely to be achieved in light of past achievements and the school's culture. In these instances, prior positive experiences by mentors was a major asset to helping new principals begin to develop appropriate reviews of the past so that the SIPAA process would be less daunting toward the end of the school year, after achievement scores were received. Coaches/mentors also were viewed as helpful by new principals in developing their SIPAA for the next school year. Again, experienced principals were able to assist novices in planning ways of involving staff members, parents, and Local School Council members in the review of past data and the planning for future improvement.

Quality of Mentoring Interactions. The perceptions of mentors and novices regarding the quality of mentoring and coaching activity increased over the 3 years of ELIS. While the majority of mentors during Year I seemed to have been admired for their work with their mentees, there were several cases where new principals expressed the belief that they had gained nothing from their mentors. Numerous comments from new principals indicated they received little or no help from experienced principals who had been assigned to serve as their mentors for the year. For example, one beginning principal asked her mentor to never return to her school after two meetings early in the school year where she had to "endure several war stories that were filled with pointless descriptions of some of the past central office administrators in Chicago."

In addition to being more selective in the choice of mentors, feedback from mentees was responsible for modifying the structure of the program. In Year I, mentors and mentees rarely came together in a large, collegial group. The only times during the first year when all mentors and mentees were encouraged, but not required, to attend sessions was at a day of small-group presentations regarding mentoring during the summer before the school year began and at a session devoted to research presentations. At no time during these two sessions were activities conducted to promote discussions among mentors and mentees.

In Years II and III, however, beginning principals and mentors came together throughout the year. Although these sessions were difficult to coordinate because of the sheer numbers of individuals involved, beginning with the Summer Mentoring Institutes in 2006 and 2007, sessions were deliberately designed with two goals in mind. One was to enable principals and mentors to get to know each other as well as many other mentors and new principals from across CPS. Small-group conversations were carried out in all settings. The second goal was to enable all participants to have a greater voice in the activities of each session. As the data-collection processes continued in each year and project participants were asked to identify the strengths and limitations of the program, there was a noticeable reduction in the number of negative comments made by the mentees. The efforts made by the OPPD design team appeared to be effective in creating a more positive learning climate.

DOES MENTORING PROMOTE INSTRUCTIONAL LEADERSHIP DEVELOPMENT?

The ELIS Project was intended to do much more than simply provide resources so that a support network for new principals could be formed. There was an expectation that the definition of school-based leadership would be changed to ensure principals fulfilled their roles as instructional leaders.

Regardless of prior experiences, all first-year principals in Chicago were provided with mentoring or coaching as a way to ensure that new principals would be instructional leaders. However, this expectation did not always materialize. The choice of new principals in Chicago is not a matter controlled only by the administration of the district. The hiring of principals is the duty of LSCs composed of elected representatives drawn from the communities serving each of the city's 700 schools. The responsibilities of CPS, through the work of the OPPD, are to provide data concerning potential candidates for the principalship who had been listed as eligible candidates. In Chicago, the selection of principals is a completely site-based process. When openings occur, eligible applicants apply directly to the LSC of an individual school. At that point, LSCs select candidates based on the specific criteria they have identified as critical for the success of their individual schools. If an LSC is seeking a strong building manager with proven experience in carrying out the oversight of budget and student discipline, members will likely not be swayed by the fact that an applicant had participated in a preservice internship that focused on curriculum renewal, staff development, change, transformational leadership and many of the skills often associated with instructional leadership.

The long-standing observation that principals can increase student learning seems well founded through a review of numerous studies. Mackey and colleagues (2006) identified apparent links between influence by principals and increases in elementary student reading scores resulting from principals' impact on teacher self-esteem, job satisfaction, and opportunities to engage in decision making related to instructional practice. Harchar and Hyle (1996) discovered that effective instructional leaders in elementary schools made extensive use of collaborative power to increase trust, respect, and collegiality in a school, and these characteristics were directly related to increased student achievement levels. Connections between how principals' relationships with staff and more effective student outcomes also has been documented (Heck, 1992; Robinson, Lloyd, & Rowe, 2008).

Further evidence of the effects that principals have on student learning was provided by Robinson and Timperley (2007) who found that the impact of principal leadership on student learning was based on five specific strategies culled from several studies of leadership and student learning and that are utilized by effective instructional leaders. These are (1) developing teaching skill in the school, (2) providing direction with clear goal setting, (3) ensuring strategic alignment between instructional content and instructional techniques, (4) creating a sense of community for student success, and (5) engaging staff in constructive conversations to solve educational problems. They also noted that instructional leaders are aware of a variety of instructional techniques ("smart tools") that can be offered to teachers as ways of addressing specific learning needs. Heck and Hallinger (2009) recently discovered that relying on more inclusive leadership behaviors, such as distributed leadership (Spillane, 2006), has been demonstrated in schools with increased levels of student achievement and growth in mathematics.

These studies reveal that proactive instructional leadership is an important contributor to increasing student achievement. This helps in identifying how principals may lead learning and not simply fit a "instructional leadership" description, which is often a vague and ambiguous term (Fulmer, 2006; Harchar & Hyle, 1996; King, 2002). Over the years, research on instructional leadership has suggested the need for principals to teach classes each day, be experts in curriculum theory and development, be strong statisticians and researchers, and spend most of their time watching teachers conduct lessons. However, it may be that instructional leadership may be largely the ability of the principal to create a culture where teachers feel as if they are trusted, respected, and able to make use of their talents while working with learners.

The challenge facing mentoring programs is how to identify ways in which the interactions between mentors and beginning principals can serve as the basis for developing knowledge, skills, and attitudes in novices so that a more collegial work environment might be created in schools. In turn, that may be the most critical skill of anyone serving in the role of true instructional leadership. Recent research may provide a more positive alternative to the image of the mentor as the experienced administrator cast as a reactor to the concerns and problems of the newcomer. The fact that there is some clarity in the knowledge base associated with instructional leadership behaviors may mean that mentoring programs for principals may experience an important transition that not only builds the capabilities of inexperienced school principals, but also impacts the learners in schools. No longer will mentors be consultants called upon to provide answers to the principals with whom they work; they need to be teachers of important skills known to have an impact on the learning of students.

The ELIS Project demonstrated that simply talking about instructional leadership and discussing the CPS Competencies did not always redefine the principal's role as more than a building manager. Because coaches during Year III were assigned multiple new principals with whom to work, there were more instances where small-group discussions were taking place. Group development was being used as a supportive strategy in many cases, and comments made by first-year principals indicated an increased effort to make use of collegial problem solving in some schools. Much of the literature related to professional development of principals as instructional leaders has noted the principal's ability to lead consensus-building discussions related to student learning is a key ingredient in effective schools (Hobson, 2003; Hoerr, 1996; Katelle, 2006; Rafforth & Foriska, 2006; Robinson & Timperley, 2007). As the ELIS Project evolved, coaches were no longer "telling" others what to do with their problems; they were deliberately making use of more facilitative and collaborative actions in their work. As a consequence, beginning principals indicated that they were making use of these same facilitative strategies when working with their teachers. Since collaboration with teachers and the establishment of collegial trust are identified as keys to a culture of more effective organizations (Riggins-Newby & Zarlengo, 2003; Sebring & Bryk, 2000), it may be inferred that behavior on the part of coaches has the potential of having an affect on the effectiveness of schools.

The observations from the ELIS Project are initial indicators of the ways in which mentoring activities might result in more effective teaching and learning. There are miles to go before one might hypothesize any direct relationship with what mentors do (or do not do) and learning by students. However, there is indeed potential to be realized through mentoring support beyond simply showing nebulous "support" for newcomers to organizations. Having a mentor does not create an effective principal overnight, particularly if effectiveness is defined as rapid increases in student achievement scores on standardized tests. But if there is patience and recognition that principals who are more comfortable with working with teachers, parents, and others, there may be strong improvement in the quality of teaching and learning. Coaches and mentors who model effective teaching strategies as they serve new principals may be leaving a long-lasting legacy on new principals who may use similar techniques with their own staffs. And that may be the real long-term benefit to new principals who not only survive, but learn how to lead.

APPENDIX A

Principal Mentoring Quality Assurance Reflection Instrument

1. **Quality Assurance Items**
   How well is mentoring helping the new principal to develop ...

   - ... in identified areas for targeted growth in the CPS Principal Competencies?

   How well is mentoring support enabling the new principal to ...

   - ... effectively address targeted academic needs expressed in the SIPAA (School Improvement Plan for Academic Achievement)?
   - ... foster a professional climate focused on student learning?

   How well do the mentoring interactions contribute to ...

   - ... reflective dialogue about professional practices?
   - ... fostering a relationship of trust?
   - ... building a deeper understanding of the work of a principal as aligned with the CPS Principal Competencies?

2. **In what areas for supporting new principal development would you most benefit from additional mentoring inservice?**

   (a) What additional development and support do you need from the district?
   (b) From your mentor?

3. **For mentors:**

   Please answer each of the following:

   Mentor Principal Goals (July, January, and May meetings)

   How well have you been able to apply content from the Mentor Principal Institute sessions in ...

   - ... aligning mentoring support to the CPS Principal Competencies?
   - ... utilizing Zachary's four phases of the mentoring relationship to target types of support?
   - ... utilizing Zachary's *Mentor's Guide* exercises and resources provided by OPPD?

APPENDIX B

Mentoring Impact Instrument

I.   Questions asked of mentors/coaches and new principals during the first term of 2006–07 and 2007–08

Questions for mentors

1.   How much influence have you had on your protégée's *thinking* about articulating a belief system through voice and action? Please describe how your protégée's thinking has been affected.

2.   How much influence have you had on your protégée's *actions* about articulating a belief system through voice and actions? Please describe how your protégée's actions have been affected.

3.   What have you done to facilitate your protégée's thinking and actions about articulating a belief system through voice and action?

4.   How much influence have you had on your protégée's *thinking* about balancing management? Please describe how your protégée's thinking has been affected.

5.   How much influence have you had on your protégée's *actions* about balancing management? Please describe how your protégée's actions have been affected.

6.   What have you done to facilitate your protégée's thinking and actions about balancing management?

Questions for new principals

1.   How much influence has your mentor had on your *thinking* about articulating a belief system through voice and action? Please describe how your thinking has been affected.

2.   How much influence has your mentor had on your *actions* about articulating a belief system through voice and action? Please describe how your actions have been affected.

3.   What has your mentor done to affect your thinking and actions about articulating a belief system through voice and action?

4.   How much influence has your mentor had on your *thinking* about balancing management? Please describe how your thinking has been affected.

5.   How much influence has your mentor had on your *actions* about balancing management? Please describe how your actions have been affected.

6. What has your mentor done to affect your thinking and actions about balancing management?

II. **Questions asked of mentors/coaches and new principals during the second and third terms of 2006–07 and 2007–08**

Questions for mentors

1. How much influence have you had on your protégée's *thinking* about assessing the quality of classroom instruction? Please describe how your protégée's thinking has been affected.

2. How much influence have you had on your protégée's *actions* about assessing the quality of classroom instruction? Please describe how your protégée's actions have been affected.

3. What have you done to facilitate your protégée's thinking and actions about assessing the quality of classroom instruction?

4. How much influence have you had on your protégée's *thinking* about engaging and developing faculty? Please describe how your protégée's thinking has been affected.

5. How much influence have you had on your protégée's *actions* about engaging and developing faculty? Please describe how your protégée's actions have been affected.

6. What have you done to facilitate your protégée's thinking and actions about engaging and developing faculty?

7. How much influence have you had on your protégée's *thinking* about facilitating and motivating change? Please describe how your protégée's thinking has been affected.

8. How much influence have you had on your protégée's *actions* about facilitating and motivating change? Please describe how your protégée's actions have been affected.

9. What have you done to facilitate your protégée's actions and thinking about facilitating and motivating change?

Questions for new principals

1. How much influence has your mentor had on your *thinking* about assessing the quality of classroom instruction? Please describe how your thinking has been affected.

2. How much influence has your mentor had on your *actions* about assessing the quality of classroom instruction? Please describe how your actions have been affected.

3. What has your mentor done to facilitate your thinking and actions about assessing the quality of classroom instruction?

4. How much influence has your mentor had on your *thinking* about engaging and developing faculty? Please describe how your thinking has been affected.

5. How much influence has your mentor had on your *actions* about engaging and developing faculty? Please describe how your actions have been affected.

6. What has your mentor done to facilitate your thinking and actions about engaging and developing faculty?

7. How much influence has your mentor had on your *thinking* about facilitating and motivating change? Please describe how your thinking has been affected.

8. How much influence has your mentor had on your *actions* about facilitating and motivating change? Please describe how your thinking has been affected.

9. What has your mentor done to facilitate your thinking and actions about facilitating and motivating change?

REFERENCES

Anderson, P. K. (2001). But what if…: Supporting leaders and learners. *Phi Delta Kappan, 82*(10), 737.

Austin, G. (1979). Exemplary schools and the search for effectiveness. *Educational Leadership, 37*(1), 10–14.

Barnett, B., & Daresh, J. (2007). *Report on the coaching impact instruments by coaches and first-year principals.* Unpublished report, Chicago Public Schools.

Bloom, G., Castagna, C., Moir, E., & Warren, B. (2005). *Blended coaching: Skills and strategies to support principal development.* Thousand Oaks, CA: Corwin Press.

Bolam, R., McMahon, A., Pocklington, K., & Weindling, D. (1995). Mentoring for new headteachers: Recent British experience. *Journal of Educational Administration, 33*(5), 29–44.

Crow, G., & Matthews, J. (1993). *Finding one's way: How mentoring can lead to dynamic leadership.* Thousand Oaks, CA: Corwin Press.

Cunat, M. B., & Daresh, J. (2007). *Mentoring for beginning urban school principals: A quality assurance process.* Paper presented at the annual meeting of the American Educational Research Association, Chicago.

Daresh, J. (1986). Support for beginning principals: First hurdles are the highest. *Theory Into Practice, 25*(3), 148–161.

Daresh, J. C. (2004). Mentoring school leaders: Professional promise or predictable problems? *Educational Administration Quarterly, 40*(4), 468–494.

Daresh, J., Best, R., Shay, L., & Alexander, M. (2008). *From mentoring to coaching: Finding the right path to support new principals.* Paper presented at the annual meeting of the American Educational Research Association, New York.

Daresh, J., & Playko, M. (1991). *The professional development of school administrators: Preservice, induction, and inservice applications.* Boston: Allyn & Bacon.

Daresh, J., & Playko, M. (1992). Perceived benefits of a preservice administrative mentoring program. *Journal of Personnel Evaluation in Education, 6,* 15–22.

Edmonds, R. (1981). Making public schools effective. *Social Policy, 12,* 56–60.

Fink, E., & Resnick. L. (2001). Developing principals as instructional leaders. *Phi Delta Kappan, 82*(8), 598–601.

Fulmer, C. (2006). Becoming instructional leaders: Lessons learned from instructional leadership work samples. *Educational Leadership and Administration, 18,* 109–122.

Harchar, R., & Hyle, A. (1996). Collaborative power: A grounded theory of administrative instructional leadership in the elementary school. *Journal of Educational Administration, 34*(3), 15–29.

Hart, A. W. (1993). *Principal succession: Establishing leadership in schools.* Albany: State University of New York Press.

Heck, R. (1992). Principals' instructional leadership and school performance implications for policy development. *Educational Evaluation and Policy Analysis, 14*(1), 21–34.

Heck, R., & Hallinger, P. (2009). Assessing the contribution of distributed leadership to school improvement and growth in match achievement. *American Educational Research Journal, 46*(3), 659–689.

Hobson, A. (2003). *Mentoring and coaching for new leaders.* Nottingham, UK: National College for School Leadership.

Hoerr, T. (1996). Collegiality: A new way to define instructional leadership. *Phi Delta Kappan, 77*(5), 380–381.

Holcomb, E. (1989). Beginning principals' perceptions of support provided during the first year of service. *ERS Spectrum, 7,* 10–16.

Katelle, D. (2006). The role of dialogue in principal support. *Leadership, 35*(5), 32-33.

King, D. (2002). Beyond instructional leadership: The changing shape of leadership. *Educational Leadership, 59*(8), 61–63.

Lindley, F. A. (2005). *The portable mentor* (2nd ed.). Thousand Oaks, CA: Corwin Press.

Lipham, J. (1981). *Effective principals, effective schools.* Reston, VA: National Association of Secondary School Principals.

Mackey, B., Pitcher, S., & Decman, J. (2006). The influence of four elementary principals upon their schools' reading programs and students' reading scores. *Education, 127*(1), 39–48.

McGhee, M., & Nelson, S. (2005) Sacrificing leaders: Villaininzing leadership: How accountability policies impair school leadership. *Phi Delta Kappan, 86*(5), 367–369.

Pocklington, K., & Weindling, D. (1996). Promoting reflection on headship through the mentoring mirror. *Educational Management and Administration, 24*(2), 175–191.

Portin, B., & Shen, J. (1998). The changing principalship: Its current status, variability, and impact. *Journal of Leadership Studies, 5*(3), 93–99.

Rafforth, M. A., & Foriska, T. (2006). Administrator participation in promoting effective problem-solving teams. *Remedial and Special Education, 27*(3), 130–134.

Reitzug, R., & West, D. (2009). *Expanding conceptions of instructional leadership: Alignments to politics to prophecy.* Paper presented at the annual meeting of the University Council for Educational Administration, Anaheim, CA.

Riggins-Newby, C., & Zarlengo, P. (2003). *Making the case for principal mentoring.* Providence, RI: The Educational Alliance at Brown University and the National Association of Elementary School Principals.

Robinson, V. M. J., Lloyd, C., & Rowe, K. J. (2008). The impact of leadership on student outcomes: An analysis of the differential effects of leadership type. *Educational Administration Quarterly, 44*(5), 635–674.

Robinson, V., & Timperley, H. (2007). The leadership of the improvement of teaching and learning: Lessons from initiatives with positive outcomes for students. *Australian Journal of Education, 51*(3), 247–256

Sebring, P., & Bryk, A. (2000). School leadership and the bottom line in Chicago. *Phi Delta Kappan, 81*(6), 440–443.

Spillane, J. (2006). *Distributed leadership.* San Francisco: Jossey-Bass.

Tooms, A. (2003). The rookie's playbook: Insights and dirt for new principals. *Phi Delta Kappan, 83*(7), 530–533.

Walker, K., & Stott. E. (1993). Preparing for leadership in schools: The mentoring contribution. In B. J. Caldwell & E. Carter (Eds.), *The return of the mentor: Strategies for workplace learning* (pp. 77–90). London: Falmer Press.

Weindling, D., & Earley, P. (1987). *The first years.* London: Falmer Press.

Weingartner, C. (2009). *Principal mentoring: A safe, simple, and supportive approach.* Thousand Oaks, CA: Corwin Press.

Zachary, L. (2005). *Creating a mentoring climate.* San Francisco: Jossey-Bass.

ABOUT THE AUTHORS

Thomas L. Alsbury is an associate professor in the Department of Leadership, Policy, and Adult and Higher Education at North Carolina State University. He started his career as a high school biology and chemistry teacher, K-12 principal, and district leader for 18 years. As a leader, his schools achieved significant and sustained student achievement gains sustained now for over 15 years, and for which they enjoyed state and national recognition. Dr. Alsbury's research focuses on school boards, superintendents, organizational governance and district reform. He directs the UCEA Joint Center for Research on the Superintendency and District Governance; and the Innovative Leadership Academy working with district leaders in high minority, high poverty rural North Carolina districts to build capacity and sustainability for student-directed innovations.

Bruce G. Barnett is a professor in the Educational Leadership and Policy Studies Department at the University of Texas at San Antonio, having entered the professorate in 1987. Besides developing and delivering master's, certification, and doctoral programs, his research interests include leadership preparation programs, particularly cohort-based learning; mentoring and coaching; reflective practice; leadership for school improvement; school-university partnerships; and the realities of beginning principals. Recently, he has become involved in international research and program development, authoring books on school improvement; researching mentoring and coaching programs operating around the world; and presenting workshops in Australia, New Zealand, England, Ireland, and Canada. In January 2008, Bruce was appointed as the associate director of international affairs for the University Council for Educational

Administration. This role is intended to: (1) increase international cooperation and partnerships, (2) encourage international memberships in UCEA, and (3) develop international research and learning opportunities.

John C. Daresh is a professor of educational leadership at the University of Texas at El Paso. He has also served at the University of Cincinnati, The Ohio State University, and the University of Northern Colorado. Over the years, he has consulted on high school reform and administrator development at numerous universities and other agencies across the United States and abroad. He recently completed 3 years of service as the lead consultant on principal mentoring programs for the Chicago Public Schools.

Gillian Forrester is a senior lecturer in education studies in the Faculty of Education, Community and Leisure at Liverpool John Moores University, Liverpool, UK. Her main research interests are in education policy and the modernization of schools, teachers' work and professionalism, performance management and school leadership.

Bonnie C. Fusarelli is an associate professor in the Department of Educational Leadership and Policy Studies at North Carolina State University, earned her PhD in educational administration at The Pennsylvania State University. Dr. Fusarelli's research examines school leadership on three levels: the building level, (school principals and effective models of leadership preparation); the district level, (superintendents and the preparation of superintendents in both traditional and nontraditional ways); and the state level. She focuses on the politics of school improvement, educational equity, and organizational change, with a particular focus on state-level education reform and leadership for social justice. Dr. Fusarelli is the recipient of numerous teaching awards at both the K-12 and university level, and is an inductee into NC State's Academy of Outstanding Teachers. Most recently, she was the College of Education's 2009 North Carolina State University Alumni Distinguished Graduate Professor and the 2008 Outstanding Teacher Award winner.

Helen M. Gunter is professor of educational policy, leadership and management in the School of Education, University of Manchester. She has produced over 70 publications including books and papers on leadership theory and practice, and she co-edits the *Journal of Educational Administration and History*. Her work has focused education policy and the growth of school leadership where she has used Bourdieu's thinking tools to explain the configuration and development of the field. She is particularly interested in the history of the field, particularly developments in knowledge production. Recently she completed the Knowledge Production in Educational Leadership Project funded by the ESRC, where she studied the relationship between the state, public policy and knowledge, and she is currently undertaking a project on distributed leadership funded by the ESRC with her colleagues Dave Hall and Joanna Bragg.

Pamela R. Hallam is an associate professor in the Educational Leadership and Foundations Department at Brigham Young University. She currently teaches educational finance and human resource management. She is the director of the Executive School Leadership Program (ExSL), which is the department's part-time, host-district model. She started her career as a high school teacher, before becoming a middle school principal, and then moving into the district office as the director of curriculum and technology. Her areas of academic interest include the role of trust in educational leadership, educational finance, and new teacher mentoring, using qualitative methods.

Julie M. Hite is an associate professor in the Educational Leadership and Foundations Department at Brigham Young University, teaching organizational leadership and strategy in education. She received her master's degree in organizational behavior from Brigham Young University and her PhD from the University of Utah in Strategic Management with focus on entrepreneurship and social/organizational networks. Her research focuses on strategic organizational networks, resource acquisition, and organizational performance in the context of U.S. and Ugandan schools, using quantitative, qualitative, and network methods.

Steven J. Hite is professor of educational research theory and methodology at Brigham Young University. His current research and service endeavors focus on the field-based use of quantitative and qualitative research, evaluation and analysis systems to explore the factors and indicators leading to improvement of the quality, efficiency, effectiveness, and equality of educational opportunities for all individuals, families and communities—particularly those from traditionally disadvantaged conditions. Dr. Hite has worked for over a decade on various education development projects in countries in Europe, Africa, and South Asia with UNESCO's International Institute of Education Planning and the Division for Education Strategies & Capacity Building.

Theodore J. Kowalski is a professor at the University of Dayton where he holds the Kuntz family chair in educational administration. His professional publications include 29 books and over 150 book chapters, monographs and referred journal articles. A former public school teacher, principal, and district superintendent, he was dean of the Teachers College at Ball State University prior to his current position. He is editor of the *Journal of School Public Relations* and serves on the editorial boards of several other professional journals including *Educational Administration Quarterly* and the *AASA Journal of Scholarship and Practice*. He received the outstanding faculty research award from the Teachers College, Ball State University in 1993 and the Alumni Award for Outstanding Research from the University of Dayton in 2005.

Chad Lochmiller is an assistant professor in the College of Education at Washington State University. His research focuses on systems, which support the development of human resources in schools and school districts. In particular, he explores how systems support the development of leaders at the school level. He served as a researcher on a national study of education leadership commissioned by The Wallace Foundation and conducted by researchers at the Center for the Study of Teaching & Policy. Dr. Lochmiller received his PhD from the University of Washington in Seattle.

Matthew Militello is an assistant professor in the Leadership, Policy, and Adult and Higher Education Department at North Carolina State University. Prior to his academic career, Militello was a middle and high public school teacher, assistant principal, and principal in Michigan. His research focuses on developing principals' knowledge and skills in the areas of school law, school data, and collective leadership. Militello has more than 30 publications and has co-authored two books: *Leading With Inquiry and Action: How Principals Improve Teaching and Learning* (2009, Corwin Press) and "*Principals Teaching the Law: 10 Legal Lessons Your Teachers Must Know* (2010, Corwin Press).

Christopher B. Mugimu is a senior lecturer and head of the Department of Curriculum, Teaching, and Media at Makerere University's School of Education. His research focuses on educational leadership, management theory and practice, planning and evaluation, educational measurement and assessment, outcome theories, contemporary issues of pedagogy in higher education. Dr. Mugimu has directed projects involved in creating open education resources in teacher education to support preservice and in-service teachers. He has won significant external grants to support his e-learning research and work in Uganda, and collaborates with an extensive network of colleagues in the United Kingdom and United States on his projects and research.

Eddie Price is a native North Carolinian who resides in Clayton, North Carolina. He has been an administrator for 7 years, all at Clayton Middle School. Eddie is in his third year as principal, and he has been a public school educator for 19 years. He received his BA in English with a teacher certification from the University of North Carolina at Wilmington. Eddie completed his master's of administration in 2002 at North Carolina State University. He is presently a doctoral student at North Carolina State University with a research interest in the success or failure of deviant youth groups, gangs, or other microcultures typically without adult advocacy. In the 2010-2011 school year, Eddie will serve as the principal of South Johnston High School, a Johnston County high school of approximately 2,000 students.

Alan R. Shoho is a professor of educational leadership and policy studies at the University of Texas at San Antonio where he has been for the past 16 years. His research focuses on aspiring principals and assistant principals, high school social processes, and organizational cultures. He currently serves as the president for the University Council for Educational Administration (UCEA). Dr. Shoho earned his EdD at Arizona State University, MEd at the University of Hawaii, and his BSEE in electrical engineering at California State University at Fullerton. He subsequently taught high school mathematics in Hawaii before moving into higher education. He teaches graduate courses in educational leadership including introduction to school administration, supervision, internship, and a doctoral proseminar.

Michael Silver was superintendent of schools in the Tukwila School District for 17 years and is currently an associate professor in the College of Education at Seattle University. He directs the university's principal preparation program. His honors include Superintendent of the Year Award by the Washington Library Media Association (2000); Excellence in Educational Leadership Award by the University Council for Educational Administration (1998), and an A+ Award by the Washington Council for Economic Education (1992). His academic interests include: educational leadership, principal and superintendent preparation, principal induction, and school improvement. Dr. Silver received his PhD from Washington University in St. Louis.

Autumn K. Tooms is a former school principal and currently serves as professor and director of the Center for Educational Leadership at the University of Tennessee. As a researcher she works to maintain a thoughtful balance between theory and practice. Her line of inquiry is centered on the politics of school leadership with a particular focus on those who are new to the principalship and those who aspire to the position. She has written books for both practitioners and scholars and he research has been published in journals that include *Kappan, Educational Leadership, Educational Administration Quarterly* and the *Journal of School Leadership*.

Thomas P. Warren is a product of the public and private education systems in the United States. He attended public schools in New York and Colorado, and private high school in North Carolina. Tom graduated from Vanderbilt with a BA in literary theory and aesthetics in 1996. In 2000, Tom desired a career change and relocated back to North Carolina to be closer to his family and to begin a second career in education. During this time, Tom worked yearly contracts with school districts, drawing on his liberal arts background to instruct in subjects such as English, language arts, and ESL at the K-12 levels, while applying to North Carolina teaching colleges and universities. Currently, Tom is a doctoral candidate preparing a mixed-methods dissertation that focuses on early college high schools, a contemporary secondary reform model. Tom's expected date of graduation is Spring 2011, after which he intends to find work as a college professor in a research intensive CED somewhere in the United States.

Sarah Beth Woodruff currently serves as director of Ohio's Evaluation and Assessment Center for Mathematics and Science Education at Miami University, Oxford, Ohio where she is a faculty member in the departments of Teacher Education and Educational Leadership. As director of the center, she provides leadership in research design, data analysis, proposal and report development, instrument development, and all aspects of evaluation and research for large-scale, externally funded education programs and projects across the nation. Dr. Woodruff is a former high school principal and state education official. Her primary research interests include the principalship, teacher and administrator preparation and licensing policy, and practice-based research in school administration.

LaVergne, TN USA
03 September 2010
195689LV00001B/53/P